To Heaven's Rim

To Heaven's Rim

The Kingdom Poets Book of World Christian Poetry
Beginnings to 1800, in English Translation

edited by BURL HORNIACHEK

EXECUTIVE EDITOR: D. S. MARTIN

CASCADE *Books* · Eugene, Oregon

TO HEAVEN'S RIM
The Kingdom Poets Book of World Christian Poetry, Beginnings to 1800, in English
Translation

Cascade Books
An Imprint of Wipf and Stock Publishers
199 W. 8th Ave., Suite 3
Eugene, OR 97401

www.wipfandstock.com

PAPERBACK ISBN: 978-1-6667-1682-5
HARDCOVER ISBN: 978-1-6667-1683-2
EBOOK ISBN: 978-1-6667-1684-9

Cataloguing-in-Publication data:

Names: Horniachek, Burl.

Title: To Heaven's Rim : The Kingdom Poets Book of World Christian Poetry , Begin-
nings to 1800, in English Translation/ Burl Horniachek.

Description: Eugene, OR: Cascade Books, 2023 | Poiema Poetry Series | Includes
bibliographical references and index.

Identifiers: ISBN 978-1-6667-1682-5 (paperback) | ISBN 978-1-6667-1683-2 (hard-
cover) | ISBN 978-1-6667-1684-9 (ebook)

Subjects: LCSH: Poetry. | Christian poetry.

Classification: PN1010 H67 2023 (print) | PN1010 (ebook)

FEBRUARY 22, 2023 10:18 AM

Contents

Introduction

THIS ANTHOLOGY HAS ITS ORIGINS in the Kingdom Poets blog by D.S. Martin. Don had been doing great work there for several years, posting a new poem every week from a different Christian poet and thus bringing attention to the many great poets who have written about their Christian faith. However, when I began to read his blog, I noted that, with some exceptions, he did not post many poems originally written in languages other than English. After I began attending his writers' group in Brampton and began to get to know him, I started to suggest poets from many different languages, in translation. I have long had an interest in translation, ever since studying Hebrew at the University of Toronto, where I had encountered the work of Robert Alter. After seeing the long list of suggested translations in the back of Harold Bloom's *The Western Canon*, I started informally comparing different translations on my own, particularly of poetry, where it makes the most difference. So, I had a fair bit of knowledge to draw on by the time I met Don. After Don published *The Turning Aside*, his anthology of contemporary Christian poets, I realized that no one had ever done an anthology of Christian poetry from around the world in translation. I talked with Don and he thought it would be a good idea.

Most people in the English-speaking world who are interested in Christian poetry are familiar with poets such as John Donne, George Herbert, John Milton, Samuel Taylor Coleridge, Gerard Manley Hopkins, T.S. Eliot, W.H. Auden, as well as more recent figures such as Geoffrey Hill, Les Murray, R.S. Thomas and Luci Shaw, among many others. For Christian poets in other languages, they will typically also be familiar with Dante, along with perhaps one or two others, such as Petrarch or St. John of the Cross, and a few traditional hymns. However, aside from these, they will very rarely know about other Christian poets in other languages, including many who are considered among the very best, sometimes *the* best, in their own tongue. The goal of this anthology is to make English-language readers aware of these poets.

(I should note that a couple of the poets here, Guillaume de Salluste Du Bartas and Maciej Kazimierz Sarbiewski, were, in the past, immensely popular in English translation. In fact, many of Isaac Watts' well-known hymns were adapted from Sarbiewski. However, both have long since fallen out of notice among English speakers.)

On those few occasions where the English reader is likely to already know something of the poet, I have tried to draw attention to parts of their work which are not so well known. For example, with Dante, the last canto of the Paradiso is perhaps the greatest religious poetry ever written, but many are not familiar with it, as it comes at the end of a long poem which many people never finish.

Unless you count Anglo-Saxon, which at this point is essentially a different language, I have not included any poetry originally composed in English. There are already several good anthologies covering Christian poetry in English during this same time period, such as Donald Davie's *New Oxford Book of Christian Verse*, and, since space is limited, I did not want to repeat their work.

What do we mean by Christian poetry? It can be difficult to define. My first criteria here is that the poet as a person must have some apparent level of Christian belief. This means, as far as we can tell, believing in the existence of God, that Jesus was divine and that his death and resurrection were involved in the salvation of men from sin, evil and death. Furthermore, at least for the purpose of this anthology, the work itself must have some specifically Christian subject matter, such as God, Jesus, the saints, the Bible, etc. Mere moral sentiment or vague gestures toward the transcendent are not enough. Still, there is no denying that, to a certain extent, this is something of a judgment call, and that, in many cases, personal belief often has to be inferred from the work.

While I am not concerned by some degree of uncertainty of belief or departure from orthodoxy, I would not include anyone who explicitly repudiated Christianity or who identified with another religious tradition. Nor would I include someone who explicitly denied certain core beliefs of Christianity, such as the existence of God or that Jesus was divine.

Aside from those religious concerns, the main criterion for inclusion in this anthology has been literary excellence. Doubtless some eccentricities of my own interests and tastes have influenced the results, but I have not gone into this project with any specific agenda: literary, theological or otherwise. Within those very broad parameters, I have intended the anthology to be historically representative, and have not limited it to poets or poems which I think have correct theology.

The most obvious area of controversy is that of Mary. There are a lot of Marian poems in this anthology. However, I think it important to clarify just what the issues are. First, Protestants have historically objected to giving Mary any continuing role (that is, beyond bearing and giving birth to Jesus) in mediating salvation, especially the not uncommon assertion that salvation must *always* come through her ongoing mediation. Second, Protestants have objected to addressing her in prayer. These issues are connected, of course, as the reason for addressing her in prayer is frequently that she has an ongoing and essential role as mediator. The poem here which most exemplifies the first issue is François Villon's Ballade of Prayer to Our Lady:

> Your graces, Holy Dame, I hardly dare
> Think can outweigh the load of sins I bear.
> Without such graces, no soul hopes to fly
> Upward, nor merit Heaven.

For most other poems, such as Dante's Paradise Canto 33 or Petrarch's poem 366, the main problem is simply that Mary is being addressed in prayer at all. I do not mean to minimize the seriousness of these theological issues: even Erasmus complained, rightly I think, that prayers to Mary and the saints had come to vastly outnumber prayers to Jesus himself. However, Protestants should at least note that most of the imagery applied to Mary in these poems is often not objectionable in itself, even from a more stringent Protestant perspective. As Sebastian Brock writes of Jacob of Serug:

> [Mary] is always regarded in relationship to the Incarnation and never *in vacuo.* In Orthodox icons the virgin is normally depicted with the incarnate Christ in her arms, symbolic of her role of co-operation with the divine economy; although the Syriac-speaking churches in fact do not make great use of icons, this iconographical tradition admirably exemplifies their Christocentric approach. And Mary's relationship to the Holy Spirit is always clear cut: the Holy Spirit is essentially the Sanctifier, while Mary is the sanctified, *par excellence.*[1]

1. Sebastian Brock, "Introduction" to Jacob of Serug, On the Mother of God, trans. Mary Hansbury. Chrestwood, NY, SVS Press, 1998, 14.

In other words, as Jacob and others here emphasize, Mary, in relation to God, is always the *receptacle* for divine grace. Much can be learned about incarnational theology from these poems, even if one ultimately objects to the context. For those who remain skeptical, I would note that there is a significant decline in Marian poetry in the second half of this anthology, even among the mostly Catholic poets there, and that this is not an artefact of my own selection process.

Another issue is when a particular poet is seen as engendering heresy and division by another tradition. The most obvious example is Martin Luther. While there is no doubt that Luther believed in God, in Christ's divinity and in his central role in salvation from sin and death, there is also no denying that, from a Roman Catholic perspective, Luther is perhaps the arch-schismatic. One can perhaps more easily overlook theological differences with later followers, but it is far more difficult with the originator himself. Still, however much distaste a more stringent Catholic may have for Luther's life and work, it is difficult to deny that he was a Christian in at least a broad sense. Thus, aside from being myself largely sympathetic to his theological leanings, I have felt no hesitation in including him. As well, "A mighty fortress is our God," the hymn I have included here, has even made its way into use among at least some Catholics.

I have also not excluded anyone for immoral behavior. While many of the poets here are rightly regarded as saints, others were seriously flawed in ways both known and unknown. Perhaps the most notorious offender here is François Villon, who engaged in various violent and criminal enterprises throughout his life. This is compounded by an undernote of self-pity in his work, a tendency to put the blame on others for his misdeeds, rather than to offer full contrition for his sins. Several others, such as Petrarch, Dafydd ap Gwilym, Pierre de Ronsard, Luís de Camões and Lope de Vega, apparently engaged in sexual activity outside marriage throughout their lives, though most are thought to have eventually stopped. In a few other cases, poets may have outright advocated for sexual arrangements widely seen as immoral among Christians. Though we don't have much information about his life, the Archpriest of Hita writes about various love affairs in an apparently autobiographical manner and some have speculated that he was an advocate for clerical concubinage. It is also unclear whether Tommaso Campanella was expressing his own preferences when he has his utopia, The City of the Sun, hold all women, like everything else, in common. On a much pettier level, Luis de Góngora and Francisco de Quevedo notoriously engaged in a long and vicious literary feud. I suspect they were not alone in such personal failings. Doubtless many of the poets here also held various social, religious and political views which many modern people might find offensive. Those views are not much represented in the poems here, though some might find Tasso's celebration of the First Crusade in *Jerusalem Delivered* problematic.

I have tried to cover all the major languages of Europe and of any other places where there were significant numbers of Christians. Still, the vast majority of the poets here are from Europe. That simply reflects where the geographic center of Christianity was for most of its first 1800 years. I did not deliberately try to make this anthology ethnically or linguistically diverse. Nonetheless, Christianity came out of the Ancient Near East and there have always been other significant pockets of Christian civilization outside Europe. Accordingly, I have ended up including a significant number poets from elsewhere. If you count the two Syriac poets, the two Armenian poets, the two Ethiopian poets, the one Chinese poet and the one Filipino poet, there are eight. If, among named poets, you add Sor Juana from Mexico and the three Greek language poets from Syria, you end up with twelve, though arguably those latter are still operating within a European cultural ambit.

If we look at the poets over time, some interesting patterns emerge. Sixteen of the poets here are from before the Great Schism of 1054. Of these, two wrote in Syriac, five in Greek, five in Latin, one in Armenian, one in Geʽez, one in Irish and one in Old English. The still relatively unified Christian tradition had comparatively equal Greek, Latin and Syriac branches, with significant offshoots in places like Armenia and Ethiopia. Northern Europe, especially England and Ireland, would eventually also begin to make contributions.

Thirteen poets come between the Great Schism and the Protestant Reformation. One wrote in Armenian, one in Irish, two in Latin, three in Italian, two in Spanish, one in Welsh, one in French, one in Geʽez and one in Croatian. The Western Catholic tradition was beginning to be dominant, but significant work was still being done in Armenia and Ethiopia. Poetry among the Eastern Orthodox was in decline.

Thirty-four poets, the majority, come from after the Protestant Reformation. Four wrote in Italian, four in German, four in French, seven in Spanish, one in Portuguese, two in Polish, one in Greek, one in Latin, one in Hungarian, one in Dutch, two in Czech, one in Chinese, one in Danish, one in Tagalog, two in Welsh and one in Russian. Of these, twenty-five were Catholic, seven Protestant, one Orthodox and one uncertain. (No one know for sure whether the author of the Cretan *Sacrifice of Abraham* was Orthodox or Catholic.) Accordingly, most explicitly religious poetry in Europe was being written by Catholics (though there would be a bit more balance if you included the English). As well, Christianity had begun to spread around the world and people from those places were beginning to make their own literary responses to the faith.

Of the named poets, fifty-five are men and four are women. Four are anonymous. All of the women I have included wrote during or after the Renaissance and Reformation, though there were notable women Christian poets before.

One might wonder why some languages and some areas of the world are not represented. In several cases, Christian cultural vitality and innovation were suppressed by Islamic hegemony. In Arabic, there was the occasional well-known Christian poet, such as Al-Akhtal, who, though he would occasionally allude to the Bible or Christian liturgical practices, did not himself write religious verse. Bulgaria was the first Slavic nation to become Christian, and, indeed, the Old Church Slavonic often used for liturgy in Slavic countries is a form of Bulgarian. However, while there were, accordingly, some medieval hymns in the language, which I chose not to include, once Bulgaria came under Muslim rule, literary culture in Bulgarian effectively ceased to exist.

A lot of high-quality poetry was written before 1800 in the closely related languages of Occitan, Catalan and Valencian, but notable religious poetry would only emerge in the 19th century. Important poets such as Ausiàs March (1400 – 1459) may have written some religious verse, but it was not among their best.

The most prominent genre of poetry in Old East Slavic (sometimes called Old Russian) was the oral folk epic. These narrative poems often featured incidental Christian elements mingled with paganism, but were not primarily religious in content. Christian religious poetry would not emerge in descendant languages such as Modern Russian and Ukrainian until the 18th and 19th centuries. Many other parts of Northern, Central and Eastern Europe had similar stories: mostly oral folk poetry for many centuries, with literate Christian poetry only emerging later, sometimes as early as the 15th century, but sometimes as late as the early 20th.

I could perhaps have looked more diligently at the smaller languages of Europe. In this case, Irish and Welsh no doubt benefitted from being so close to the English geographically. While I have included work originally written in Old English, I have not included anything from works such as Pearl, Langland or Chaucer in Middle English. Though there have been translations of these works, they are still often read in the original.

I have tried to include poetry from Ethiopia, which has been largely Christian since the 300s, including excerpts from St. Yared and a selection from *The Harp of Glory* by Hensa Krestos. However, the work of many of Ethiopia's greatest religious poets, including that of Yohannis Geblawi, Tewaney, and Kifle Yohannis, exists only in oral form and has never been written down. It was simply not practical to travel to Ethiopia to collect these poems for translation, especially in the midst of a pandemic.

Greek poetry flourished under the Byzantine Empire, and two great poets, St. John of Damascus and St. Cosmas of Maiuma, would continue to write in Greek even under early Islamic rule in Syria-Palestine. However, with the reduced fortunes of the Byzantine Empire, Greek poetry would also decline in quality. The poetry of St. Symeon the New Theologian, for example, has real artistic value, but is not on the level of Romanos, John of Damascus or Cosmas. New poetry then largely ceased to exist after the Empire was overrun. A notable exception was the Cretan Renaissance, which took place under renewed Christian rule by the Venetians. This relatively short cultural moment coincided with the Renaissance in the West and produced major poets, such as Vitsentzos Kornaros, and painters, such as El Greco.

Latin poetry during the Christian era remains strangely underexplored and undertranslated. I have included several Latin hymns from the Early Church up through the Middle Ages, and have included one Neo-Latin poet in Maciej Kazimierz Sarbiewski.

As we are going to press, I have been made aware of other poets that I probably should have included, particularly from Spanish and Danish. There are doubtless even more in other languages. A book like this can never claim to be definitive.

An interesting question is what purpose these works were created for. About a third of were intended for or adapted to use in the liturgy. Broadly there are two main liturgical genres. The works of St. Ephrem, Jacob of Serug and St. Romanos the Melodist are verse sermons, while those of St. Ambrose, Prudentius, St. Yared, St. Venantius Fortunatus, St. John of

Damascus, St. Cosmas of Maiouma, St. Thomas Aquinas, Martin Luther, Paul Gerhardt, Thomas Kingo, William Williams Pantycelyn and Ann Griffiths, as well as anonymous pieces like the Akathistos Hymn and the Stikhera for the Last Kiss, are hymns. Others, such as Sedulius or Arnulf of Leuven, have had their work excerpted and adapted for use as hymns. Much of the liturgical work tends to come towards the beginning of the Christian era, with most of the new liturgical work since the Reformation by Protestants.

The other two thirds or so of the work here is intended for private devotion or edification. The sheer number of genres represented is astounding: lyrics, philosophical poems, mystical poems, didactic poems, tragedies, epics and comic poems. Christian poets have approached their faith from an almost bewildering number of perspectives.

I have preferred translations which preserve at least something of the original form. At its minimum, this means that if the original is in meter, the translation is also in meter (acknowledging, of course, that metrical systems differ from language to language). If there is rhyme, the translation may keep that too, as most here do, but this is not as important as meter. In some cases it would be simply impossible to retain the rhyme. For example, Nerses' *Jesus the Son* is made up of long sections of monorhyme, something impossible to replicate in English. The terza rima of Dante is not quite as unworkable, but is still very difficult. But, even in cases where keeping the rhyme is possible, the translator may choose not to. Michael Smith's Quevedo and Edith Grossman's Sor Juana are superb translations which retain only meter. Though not as common, there are also a few cases, such as Christopher Childers' St. John of Damascus and St. Cosmas, where the translator has used rhyme to translate an unrhymed original. While not what I usually prefer, there is ample precedent for this in the English tradition, and the results, as here, are often excellent. I tend to avoid translations of formal poetry into free verse. Still, there are exceptions. Jan Zwicky's renditions of Vittoria Colonna are clearly the best available and are great poetry in themselves. With a few others, such as the Syriac poets, the meaning of the unrhymed original has been carried over relatively straightforwardly line for line without trying to replicate the original prosody or come up with some reasonable equivalent. This can still work because the original is informed by Biblical parallelism. Very rarely, as with Gregory of Narek's Lamentations, the original itself does not have regular meter or rhyme to preserve.

For the most part, I have stuck to already available translations. However, there were a few times when I commissioned new ones. In almost all cases, the poet or poem already had an extremely high reputation in its original language, and was thus a pretty safe bet. Sometimes, there was an English translation which could tell me whether there was "something there." All of the new translators are people with an impressive track record as poets and translators of poetry, and I tried to pair them with material that matched both their skills and their sensibility. In most cases, they were also highly competent in their source languages. However, in a few instances, I could not find someone with both the poetic skill and the linguistic competency I wanted. In those cases, I paired someone who knew the original language with American poet Rhina Espaillat to create a team translation. In a few other cases, such as with The Dream of the Rood or Catharina Regina von Greiffenberg, new translations had already been done, but had not been previously published. In many cases, these works have never before been translated into English.

Most of the already previously published translations come from the 20th century. However, some are earlier. Josuah Sylvester's translation of Du Bartas was immensely popular in the early 17th century, but then fell out of favor. Henry Vaughan is a famous poet from the 17th century, while Henry Wadsworth Longfellow and Gerard Manley Hopkins are from the 19th. Many of the hymns were translated by various 19th century ministers, with Latin tending to be translated by high church Anglicans and German by Non-conformists.

In one case, Mark DeGarmeaux added some missing stanzas to an earlier translation of Thomas Kingo by J.A. Jeffrey. Stanzas 1, 2, 6, 7, 12 and 13 are by Jeffrey and the remaining by DeGarmeaux. Henry W. Baker did the same to an earlier translation of Prudentius by J.M. Neale.

I have aimed to introduce readers to this body of poetry as enjoyable English poetry. While I have tried to avoid translations which grossly misrepresent the original, I make no pretensions to scholarly accuracy. That said, I do hope this book will help scholars get a sense of the broad sweep of Christian poetry outside the English-speaking world.

Readers should not assume that titles go back to the original author. Some do originate with the author, but others are traditional or added by the translator. Sometimes, they are simply the first line of the poem. With some exceptions, I have typically used whatever the translator used.

I have mostly not included any notes. For background, all the reader really needs is a reasonable familiarity with the Bible. A bit of training in philosophy and theology might be helpful, but is mostly unnecessary. The very few references which remain obscure can be looked up on Wikipedia or elsewhere on the internet. The only item in this anthology which might cause real difficulty is the excerpt from Sor Juana's *First Dream*, and, if anyone finds it too obscure, they can look at Alan S. Trueblood's excellent prose summary on page 169 of his *A Sor Juana Anthology* (Harvard, 1990).

I would like to thank all those who contributed new translations: Ralph Lee (Yared), Christopher Childers (John of Damascus, Cosmas of Maiuma), Scott Cairns (Stikhera for the Last Kiss), Anthony M. Esolen (The Dream of the Rood), Rhina P. Espaillat (The Archpriest of Hita, Dafydd ap Gwilym, Marulić, Bridel, Belén), Rowan Williams (Dafydd ap Gwilym), Joseph S. Salemi (Villon), Henry C. Cooper (Marulić, Bridel), Richard Jones (Petrarch), Clive Lawrence (Ronsard), A.E. Stallings (The Sacrifice of Abraham), the team of Sarah Klassen, Joanne Epp and Sally Ito (Greiffenberg) and René B. Javellana (Belén).

I would also like to thank Daniel Cowper, Scott Cairns, Jack Mitchell, Aaron Poochigian, Jane Greer, Rhina Espaillat and Alice Major for a quick last minute Twitter-and-email workshop of my versions of Yared.

I would also like to thank those who played a supporting role in the translation process: Dana Gioia for helping me get in touch with Rhina Espaillat and A.E. Stallings (as well as for general support), David Yezzi for helping me get in touch with Christopher Childers, Gwyneth Lewis for looking over Rhina and Rowan's translation of Dafydd ap Gwylim, Malcolm Guite for getting me in touch with Gwyneth, Sam Rubenson for helping me get in touch with Haileyesus Molow.

Thanks to local Winnipeg poets Sarah Klassen, Sally Ito and Joanne Epp for introducing me to Catharina Regina von Greiffenberg (and for general support).

I could not have completed this anthology without the help and advice of many scholars who took the time to respond to my emails. I would like to thank Gordon Zerbe, John McGuckin, and Andrew Louth for advice on Patristic Greek poetry, Anthony Esolen for advice on Latin poetry (and for general support), David Holton, Wim Bakker and Dia Philippides for advice on Cretan Renaissance Greek poetry, James Partridge and Marie Škarpová for advice on Czech and Slovak poetry, Samer Mahdy Ali for advice on Arabic poetry, Heather McHugh and and Nikolai Popov for advice on Bulgarian poetry, Amsalu Tefera and Haileyesus Molow for advice on Geʿez poetry and Victoria Moul for advice on Neo-Latin poetry.

Of all the many resources I consulted, by far the most valuable was the *Princeton Book of World Poetries*, edited by Roland Greene and Stephen Cushman.

I would like to thank the following individual translators, literary executors and publishers for their special generosity with permissions: George Szirtes, Anthony Mortimer, Jonathan Chaves, Thomas J. Samuelian, Mark DeGarmeaux, Scott Cairns, Rhina Espaillat, Anthony Esolen, Sarah Klassen, Sally Ito, Joanne Epp, Hallie O'Donovan, Christopher Wilbur, Margaret Clewett, Luis Ingelmo, Alexander Levitsky, Maryann Corbett, E.J. Hutchinson, Michigan Slavic Publications, Corvina Press, St. Vladimir's Seminary Press, the Armenian Institute and Paraclete Press.

As well, I was encouraged by the very enthusiastic responses to this project from William Baer, Rowan Williams and Sherry Roush.

I would like to thank my wife Angela for all her support, as well as my parents for indulging my artistic predilections over the years.

However, the two individuals besides myself who are by far the most responsible for the creation of this book, my co-conspirators as it were, are Don Martin and Rhina Espaillat. I would like to thank Don especially for the opportunity to publish this book, as well as his patience and unwavering support throughout the many ups and downs in my own life and in the world these past few years. I would like to thank Rhina for the extraordinary amount of skill, effort and enthusiasm she has put into the translations here and for being an absolute delight to work with.

If I have forgotten anyone, my sincere apologies. Any mistakes here are my own.

Burl Horniachek
Selkirk, Manitoba, Canada
2023

ST. EPHREM THE SYRIAN (c. 306–373) was a Syrian theologian and poet. He was born in Nisibis (modern-day Nusaybin, Turkey) and lived most of his life in Edessa. He died ministering to victims of the plague.

_____

HYMNS ON PARADISE

XII

1. There sprang up within me a query
    that troubled my thoughts;
I wished to make enquiry,
    but was afraid of being importunate.
But the moment God perceived
    what lay in my thoughts
He enveloped with His wisdom
    this question of mine,
and thus I felt assured
    that in all that He told me
He had accepted my wish
    and encompassed it for me within His own words.

Response: Praise to Your grace that has compassion on sinners.

2. For He explained to me
    about the serpent,
how the truth concerning hidden things
    had reached this deceiver.
It was by listening that he learned
    and imagined he had knowledge;
the voice had cried out
    to Adam and warned him
of that Tree of knowledge
    of what is good and what evil;
the cunning one heard that voice
    and seized on its meaning.

1

3. He deceived the husbandman
    so that he plucked prematurely
the fruit which gives forth its sweetness
    only in due season
—a fruit that, out of season,
    proves bitter to him who plucks it.
Through a ruse did the serpent
    reveal the truth,
knowing well that the result
    would be the opposite, because of their presumption;
for blessing becomes a curse
    to him who seizes it in sin.

4. Remember Uzziah,
    how he entered the sanctuary;
by seeking to seize the priesthood
    he lost his kingdom.
Adam, by wishing to enrich himself,
    incurred a double loss.
Recognize in the sanctuary
    the Tree,
in the censer the fruit,
    and in the leprosy the nakedness.
From these two treasures
    there proceeded harm in both cases.

5. Abraham doubted and asked
    "How shall I know?"
He uttered what he wanted
    but found what he did not want.
God, through a few brief words,
    taught him one thing in place of another.
The same happened to Adam
    in the Garden:
he lost what he had desired,
    and found what he dreaded:
it was disgrace, instead of glory,
    that God caused the audacious man to know.

6. There came another Athlete,
   this time not to be beaten;
He put on the same armor
   in which Adam had been vanquished.
When the adversary beheld
   the armor of conquered Adam,
he rejoiced, not perceiving
   that he was being taken by surprise;
He who was within the armor would have terrified him,
   but His exterior gave him courage.
The evil one came to conquer,
   but he was conquered and could not hold his ground.

7. Observe how there too
   the evil one revealed the truth:
he recited Scripture there,
   he exacted truth there;
he clothed himself with a psalm,
   hoping to win by reciting it.
But our Lord would not listen
   to him—
not because what he said
   was untrue,
but because the evil one
   had armed himself with deception.

8. Look too at Legion:
   when in anguish he begged,
our Lord permitted and allowed him
   to enter into the herd;
respite did he ask for, without deception,
   in his anguish,
and our Lord in His kindness
   granted this request.
His compassion for demons
   is a rebuke to that People,
showing how much anguish His love suffers
   in desiring that men and women should live.

9. Encouraged by the words
     I had heard,
I knelt down and wept there,
     and spoke before our Lord:
"Legion received his request from You
     without any tears;
permit me, with my tears,
     to make my request,
grant me to enter, instead of that herd,
     the Garden,
so that in Paradise I may sing
     of its Planter's compassion.

10. Because Adam touched the Tree
     he had to run to the fig;
he became like the fig tree,
     being clothed in its vesture:
Adam, like some tree,
     blossomed with leaves.
Then he came to that glorious
     tree of the Cross,
put on glory from it,
     acquired radiance from it,
heard from it the truth
     that he would return to Eden once more.

11. Let Job uncover for you
     the impudence of Satan:
how he asks and beseeches
     the Just One for permission
to test out your minds
     in the furnace of temptation.
This is what
     the abominable one said:
"No silver without fire
     has ever been assayed;
falsehood will be put to shame,
     what is true will receive due praise.

4

12. It is written, furthermore,
     Show no favor to the rich,
do not even help out
     a poor man in court;
let not judgment be blinded
     in the eye of the scales
so that truth may be apparent
     in all things;
if it is a case of forgiveness,
     let us praise His grace,
if of punishment,
     let us acknowledge His justice."

13. Our Lord rebuked the demon
     and shut his mouth;
He was angry with the leper,
     He said "woe" to the scribes
along with the rich;
     the swine He cast into the sea,
He dried up
     the fig tree.
But all these were occasions
     for us to receive benefit,
for by their means He opened up
     the great gates of His discerning actions.

14. He did not use threats,
     but gave a rebuke in order to save;
even though He said "woe,"
     yet His nature is peaceable,
even though He rebuked the demon,
     He remains completely serene;
it was not out of anger
     that He bade the swine
be cast into the sea;
     nor was it hate which withered up
the fig at His curse,
     for He is in all things good.

15. Two Trees did God place
      in Paradise,
the Tree of Life
      and that of Wisdom,
a pair of blessed fountains,
      source of every good;
by means of this
      glorious pair
the human person can become
      the likeness of God,
endowed with immortal life
      and wisdom that does not err.

16. With that manifest knowledge
      which God gave to Adam,
whereby he gave names to Eve
      and to the animals,
God did not reveal the discoveries
      of things that were concealed;
but in the case
      of that hidden knowledge
from the stars downward,
      Adam was able to pursue
enquiry into all
      that is within this universe.

17. For God would not grant him the crown
      without some effort;
He placed two crowns for Adam,
      for which he was to strive,
two Trees to provide crowns
      if he were victorious.
If only he had conquered
      just for a moment,
he would have eaten the one and lived,
      eaten the other and gained knowledge;
his life would have been protected from harm
      and his wisdom would have been unshakable.

6

18. The Just One did not wish
     to give Adam the crown quite free,
even though He had allowed him
     to enjoy Paradise without toil;
God knew that if Adam wanted
     he could win the prize.
The Just One ardently wished
     to enhance him,
for, although the rank of supernal beings
     is great through grace,
the crown for the proper use of free will
     is by no means paltry.

19. In His justice He gave
     abundant comfort to the animals;
they do not feel shame for adultery,
     nor guilt for stealing;
without being ashamed
     they pursue every comfort they encounter,
for they are above
     care and shame;
the satisfaction of their desires
     is sufficient to please them.
Because they have no resurrection,
     neither are they subject to blame.

20. The fool, who is unwilling to realize
     his honorable state,
prefers to become just an animal,
     rather than a man,
so that, without incurring judgment,
     he may serve naught but his lusts.
But had there been sown in animals
     just a little
of the sense of discernment,
     then long ago would the wild asses have lamented
and wept at their not
     having been human.

Translated from the Syriac by Sebastian P. Brock

St. Ambrose of Milan (c. 340–397) was a Roman bishop, theologian and hymn writer. He grew up in Augusta Treverorum (present-day Trier in Germany) and was educated in Rome. He entered public service, became governor and then bishop of Mediolanum (present-day Milan), the effective capital of the Empire. He was a mentor to St. Augustine.

Maker of All, Eternal King

Maker of all, eternal King,
Who day and night about dost bring:
Who weary mortals to relieve,
Dost in their times the seasons give:

Now the shrill cock proclaims the day,
And calls the sun's awakening ray,
The wandering pilgrim's guiding light,
That marks the watches night by night.

Roused at the note, the morning star
Heaven's dusky veil uplifts afar:
Night's vagrant bands no longer roam,
But from their dark ways hie them home.

The encouraged sailor's fears are o'er,
The foaming billows rage no more:
Lo! E'en the very Church's Rock
Melts at the crowing of the cock.

O let us then like men arise;
The cock rebukes our slumbering eyes,
Bestirs who still in sleep would lie,
And shames who would their Lord deny.

New hope his clarion note awakes,
Sickness the feeble frame forsakes,
The robber sheathes his lawless sword,
Faith to fallen is restored.

Look in us, Jesu, when we fall,
And with Thy look our souls recall:
If Thou but look, our sins are gone,
And with due tears our pardon won.

Shed through our hearts Thy piercing ray,
Our soul's dull slumber drive away:
Thy Name be first on every tongue,
To Thee our earliest praises sung.

All laud to God the Father be;
All praise, Eternal Son, to Thee;
All glory, as is ever meet,
To God the Holy Paraclete. Amen.

Translated from the Latin by W.J. Copeland

AURELIUS PRUDENTIUS CLEMENS (c. 348–405/413), usually known simply as PRUDENTIUS, was a Roman poet. He was born in the province of Tarraconensis (now Northern Spain) and probably died in the Iberian Peninsula sometime after 405, possibly around 413.

OF THE FATHER'S LOVE BEGOTTEN

Of the Father's love begotten,
Ere the worlds began to be,
He is Alpha and Omega,
He the source, the ending He,
Of the things that are, that have been,
And that future years shall see,
Evermore and evermore!

At His Word the worlds were framèd;
He commanded; it was done:
Heaven and earth and depths of ocean
In their threefold order one;
All that grows beneath the shining
Of the moon and burning sun,
Evermore and evermore!

He is found in human fashion,
Death and sorrow here to know,
That the race of Adam's children
Doomed by law to endless woe,
May not henceforth die and perish
In the dreadful gulf below,
Evermore and evermore!

O that birth forever blessèd,
When the virgin, full of grace,
By the Holy Ghost conceiving,
Bore the Saviour of our race;
And the Babe, the world's Redeemer,
First revealed His sacred face,
evermore and evermore!

O ye heights of heaven adore Him;
Angel hosts, His praises sing;
Powers, dominions, bow before Him,
and extol our God and King!
Let no tongue on earth be silent,
Every voice in concert sing,
Evermore and evermore!

This is He Whom seers in old time
Chanted of with one accord;
Whom the voices of the prophets
Promised in their faithful word;
Now He shines, the long expected,
Let creation praise its Lord,
Evermore and evermore!

Righteous Judge of souls departed,
Righteous King of them that live,
On the Father's throne exalted
None in might with Thee may strive;
Who at last in vengeance coming
Sinners from Thy face shalt drive,
Evermore and evermore!

Thee let old men, Thee let young men,
Thee let boys in chorus sing;
Matrons, virgins, little maidens,
With glad voices answering:
Let their guileless songs re-echo,
And the heart its music bring,
Evermore and evermore!

Christ, to Thee with God the Father,
And, O Holy Ghost, to Thee,
Hymn and chant with high thanksgiving,
And unwearied praises be:
Honour, glory, and dominion,
And eternal victory,
Evermore and evermore!

Translated from the Latin by J. M. Neale,
extended by Henry W. Baker

SEDULIUS was a 5th century Roman poet. He was also the author of the Biblical epic *The Paschal Song* and may have lived in Italy. Little else is known about him.

A SOLIS ORTUS CARDINE

Afar from rising of the sun
Unto the limit of the earth,
The Christ, our prince, now let us sing–
His holy Mary-virgined birth.

Behold: the author of the world,
Though blessed, is clothed in slave's attire,
In order flesh by flesh to free
And save his creatures from the mire.

Concealed within the maiden's womb,
The grace of heaven enters in;
Her belly does not know it bears
The secret saving us from sin.

Domained in Mary's modesty,
God makes a temple of her breast.
How strange! Untouched, the girl brought forth
Her Son, the Word-created guest.

Ere long her labor bore the King
Whom Gabriel had once foretold,
Whom John's prenatal preaching had
Before proclaimed with leaping bold.

For, sleeping, he did not despise
To take the prickling straw as bed;
A mother's milk sustained the babe
By whom the birds of heav'n are fed.

"Good tidings!" chant celestial choirs
Of angels as God's praises ring.
To shepherds now is manifest
The Shepherd who made everything.

How, Herod, can your hostile mind
Greet his arrival with dismay?
He gives eternal realms and does
Not grasp at kingdoms of a day.

Incensed conversely Magi came,
Judea's star their mystic guide.
By light they seek the light; their gift
Declares that God with man abides.

Knave tyrant, do you hear the sound
Of mothers weeping for their dead,
The battered brood of baby boys
Whose sacrificial blood you shed?

Let down into the Jordan's flood,
The Lamb of heaven made it pure–
The Lamb who took away our sins
With Worded water as the cure.

Miraculous deeds fathered faith
His Father was not man but God,
As sickly bodies found their strength
And corpses rose up at his nod.

New kind of power! Water jars
Suddenly blush and change their hue.
At Christ's command, metamorphosed,
Unwatered wine the servants drew.

On bended knee, the captain begged
The Lord to grant health to his slave;
The ardent burning of belief
Snuffed out the fire the fever craved.

Pretending water was like rock
Stout Peter walked upon the sea;
Upheld by Christ's right hand, his faith
Made paths denied naturally.

Quartered four days now, Lazarus,
A rotting corpse, recovered life,
And, freed from fetters moribund,
Survived his death and graveyard strife.

Red rivulets of ceaseless blood
Mere contact with Christ's clothing dammed,
The sanguine flow made desiccate
By tearful faith's extended hand.

Sold out by slack recusant limbs,
Commanded suddenly to rise,
The paralytic stood and walked,
His dormant bed borne off as prize.

Then hangman Judas, by design,
Unfeeling, with a kiss betrayed
His master, simulating peace–
"Disciple" just a part he played.

Veracity Itself by lies
Was given to ungodly men
And fastened, guiltless, to a cross
With scoundrels from a robbers' den.

Xenian in their pious care,
The women brought myrrh to his tomb.
The angel told them he was gone;
He'd burst forth living from death's womb.

Ye faithful, come, and let us sing
With sweetest hymns Christ's victory,
Who, sold for silver, sacking hell,
Bought us back from sin's penalty.

Zealous for blood, the serpent's head
and lion's mouth, devouring, God's
Only-Begotten under foot
Has crushed and back to heaven trod.

Translated from the Latin by E.J. Hutchinson

ST. JACOB OF SERUG (c. 451–521) was a Syrian priest, theologian and poet. He was born in the village of Kurtam in the region of Serug and probably educated in Edessa. Near the end of his life, he was appointed bishop for the city of Batna.

THE MYSTERY OF MARY

A wonderful discourse has now moved me to speak;
you who are discerning, lovingly incline the ear of the soul!

The story of Mary stirs in me, to show itself in wonder;
you, wisely, prepare your minds!

The holy Virgin calls me today to speak of her;
let us purge our hearing for her luminous tale, lest it be dishonoured.

Second heaven, in whose womb the Lord of heaven dwelt
and shone forth from her to expel darkness from the lands.

Blessed of women, by whom the curse of the land was eradicated,
and the sentence henceforth has come to an end.

Modest, chaste and filled with beauties of holiness,
so that my mouth is inadequate to speak a word concerning her.

Daughter of poor ones, who became mother of the Lord of Kings
and gave riches to a needy world that it might live from Him.

Ship which bore treasure and blessings from the house of the Father
and came and poured out riches on our destitute earth.

Good field which, without seed, gave a sheaf
and grew a great yield while being unploughed.

Second Eve who generated Life among mortals,
and paid and rent asunder that bill of Eve her mother.

Maiden who gave help to the old woman who was prostrate;
she raised her from the Fall where the serpent had thrust her.

Daughter who wove a garment of glory and gave it to her father;
he covered himself because he was stripped naked among the trees.

Virgin who without marital union marvellously became a mother,
a mother who remained without change in her virginity.

Fair palace which the King built and entered and dwelt in it;
the doors were not opened before Him when He was going out.

Maiden who became like the heavenly chariot and solemnly
carried that Mighty One, bearing Creation.

Bride who conceived although the bridegroom had never been seen by
    her;
she gave birth to a baby without her coming to the place of his Father.

How can I form an image of this most fair one,
with ordinary colours whose mixtures are not suitable for her?

The image of her beauty is more glorious and exalted than my
    composition;
I do not dare let my mind depict the form of her image.

It is easier to depict the sun with its light and its heat
than to tell the story of Mary in its splendour.

Perhaps the rays of the sphere can be captured in pigments,
but the tale concerning her is not completely told by those who preach.

If anyone ventures, in what order can he describe her
and with what class must he mix to tell it with?

With virgins, with saints, with the chaste?
With married women, with mothers or with handmaids?

Behold the body of the glorious one carries tokens of virginity and milk,
perfect birth yet sealed womb; who is equal to her?

While it seems that she is in the company of maidens,
I see her, like a handmaid, giving milk to the lad.

While I hear that Joseph her husband dwells with her,
I behold her who is not joined in conjugal union.

While I seek to reckon her in the order of virgins,
behold the sound of birth pangs striking her, comes to me.

Because of Joseph, I think to call her a married woman,
but I believe that she has not been known by any mortal.

I see her who bears the son of a fertile mother,
yet it seems to me that she belongs in the order of virgins.

She is virgin and mother and wife of a husband yet unmated;
how may I speak if I say that she is incomprehensible?

Love moves me to speak of her, which is proper,
but the height of her discourse is too difficult for me; what will I do?

I will cry openly that I have not been fit nor am I yet,
and I will return because of love that I might recount her story which is
    exalted.

Only love does not reproach when speaking,
because its way is pleasing and enriches the one who hears it.

With wonder I will speak of Mary while I stand in awe,
because the daughter of earthly beings has ascended to such a high rank.

Now did grace itself bend down the Son to her,
or was she so beautiful that she became Mother to the Son of God?

That God descended on earth by grace is manifest,
and since Mary was very pure she received Him.

He looked on her humility and her gentleness and her purity,
and dwelt in her because it is easy for Him to dwell with the humble.

"On whom will I gaze except the gentle and humble?"
He looked on and dwelt in her because she was humble among those who
   are born.

Even she herself said that He looked on her lowliness and dwelt in her,
because of this she shall be extolled, for she was so pleasing.

Humility is total perfection,
so that when man first beholds God, then he behaves humbly.

For Moses was humble, a great one among all men;
God went down to him on the mountain in revelation.

Again humility is seen in Abraham,
for although he was just, he called himself dust and ashes.

Again also John was humble because he was so proclaiming
that he was not worthy to loose the sandals of the Bridegroom, his Lord.

By humility, the heroic in every generation have been pleasing,
because it is the great way by which one draws near to God.

But no one on earth was brought low like Mary,
and from this it is manifest that no one was exalted like her.

In proportion to lowliness, the Lord also bestows manifestation;
He made her his mother and who is like her in humility?

If there were another, purer and gentler than she,
in this one He would dwell and that one renounce so as not to dwell in her.

And if there were a soul <more> splendid and holy,
rather than hers, He would choose this one and forsake that one.

Mary, "Second Heaven"

He is great while not diminishing in his small state,
and if He had feared lest He be reduced, He would not be great.

If the small womb of Mary had not contained Him,
heaven which is greater would have held Him, and He would have been
  contained.

Because He dwelt in her womb, it is known that He is without limit;
heaven and earth are small for Him to dwell in.

If a small place had been too small for Him, and a big one too big,
He would not have been great because in a small place He would be
  contained.

And because the great heaven and a small womb are worthy of Him,
by this He makes known his incomprehensible greatness.

There is no place in the bosom of his Father which is not filled with Him,
but because He dwelt in a womb, He did not overflow from it, because He
  was filling it all.

The stretches of heaven are not vast for Him, because He is bigger than all;
the humble maiden is not small for Him because He extends and con-
  tracts Himself.

He descended and dwelt in her and her small womb was large for Him,
for a small place cannot straighten or constrain Him.

Heaven and Mary were for Him equal when He dwelt in her,
yet not equal, for to the one who beholds her Mary is greater.

Heaven is his throne and Mary his Mother and behold they are not equal,
for the throne does not resemble the Mother because the Mother is
   greater.

Heaven and Mary, singly He chose the both of them,
He made one of them a throne and the other a Mother.

I will not call heaven "Mary" lest be dishonoured
the Mother of the King by the name of his throne, and He become angry
   with me.

Now judge truly my words, O wise one,
and if it would not provoke you, explain to us who is greater.

Heaven beholds the maiden Mother and the Only-begotten;
between the two of them who is greater, and who is more blessed?

Which of them is nearer to Him and dearer to Him,
and more precious to Him and more united to Him?

Heaven did not give milk to Him who became a Babe,
but He seized the breast in the bosom of Mary who had become his
   Mother.

Heaven did not conceive Him nor bear Him nor suckle Him,
but she bore, embraced, raised Him and to her belongs a blessing.

O Mary, you are blessed among women and full of blessings
without my word laying hold of your mystery that it be contained by it.

Pure Virgin and Mother, exalted above marriage,
full of blessings for which a myriad of mouths are not adequate!

Conception is in your womb but virginity in your members;
milk is in your breasts but your womb is closed to marital coupling.

The suffering of intercourse of ordinary married women is removed
   from you,
but in your womb dwells the fruit making all mothers glad.

Your body is free from the way of coupling,
yet your womb is filled with a babe, beloved of nurturers!

A man is far, but birth without marriage is near;
on account of this the learned ones are defeated, they are not capable of
   understanding you.

O cloud of mercy, which is full of hope for all the world,
all the earth which had been ravaged was pacified by it.

O ship of riches in which the Father's treasury was sent
to the poor in a needy place and it enriched them!

O field, which without a ploughman yielded a sheaf of life,
and all creation which had been needy was satiated by it.

O virginal vine, which though not pruned gave a cluster,
behold by whose wine creation, which was mourning, rejoices.

Daughter of poor ones, who was mother to the only rich One,
Behold whose treasures are lavished on mendicants to enrich them.

She was a letter in which the secret of the Father was written
which by her flesh He revealed to the world that the world might be re-
   newed by it.

O letter—it was not a case of it being written and then sealed;
but it was sealed first and only then written—a great wonder!

For while it was sealed, it was mystically written;
although not opened, it was read clearly.

She became a letter, and what was written on her is the Word;
when it was read, the earth was enlightened by its tidings.

He stooped to lowliness because it was easy for Him,
but his greatness rushed after Him that He be honoured by it.

Translated from the Syriac by Mary T. Hansbury

St. Romanos the Melodist (late 5th-century–after 555) was a Byzantine Greek poet. He was born to a Jewish family in either Emesa (present-day Homs) or Damascus. He was ordained a deacon in Berytos (Beirut), but later moved to Constantinople, where he was a sacristan at Hagia Sophia until retiring to a nearby monastery.

THE TEMPTATION OF JOSEPH

1. Licentiousness lures the young to forbidden pleasure,
    but purity bolsters the prudent with manly courage.
When Joseph felt this tension in Egypt, he showed himself a just man:
    he trembled at the thought of sin,
because the eye that never sleeps sees everything.

II. Like Olympic athletes we have just completed the marathon of the
    Lenten fast.
    Now we eagerly toe our marks to retrace the Passion of the Lord.
Come, comrades, let us all race to equal the standard of purity set by Joseph.
As we shudder at the memory of the fig-tree cursed into sterility,
    let us also wither the desires of our flesh by works of mercy,
so, when we arrive breathless at the resurrection,
    we can anoint ourselves with forgiveness, like perfumed oil sent from
        heaven,
because the eye that never sleeps sees everything.

[III. Grant that we who have run the course of your Passion, Lord,
    may also celebrate the triumph of your resurrection.
You are our Savior and your eye never sleeps.]

I. We have a royal commander who rewards his warriors
    with the Kingdom of Heaven.
    Let us gird our souls with the impenetrable armor of virtue,
    so that, like disciplined troops, we can battle sin.

24

But what is virtue? It is revealed by philosophy,
   which tradition calls the art of arts,
   the science of sciences.
On it, as on a ladder, a soul finds hand-grips
   and scales the ramparts of heavenly life.
Philosophy teaches men wisdom and courage,
   self-control and justice.
Let our ranks be protected by such armor
   as we battle to claim Christ's favor.
He grants to those who love him
   the wreaths of triumph over his foes,
because the eye that never sleeps sees everything.

2. So that all of us can experience the dazzling splendor
   which virtue possesses and dispenses,
   let us race to take Joseph as our model
   and, paced by his purity, cherish a life fortified by philosophy.
Sold by his jealous brothers, Joseph never became a slave to passion.
   He steeled his will, made it his wise commander:
   he mastered the lures of the flesh.
He was never shaken by the blandishments of a woman.
   He deflected her flatteries with manly courage.
Her arguments blew like cyclones
   to topple the bastion of his self-control.
She poured out wine in drunken storms,
   offered rivers of gold.
But Joseph, though young, was of heroic stock
   and he stood firm on an unshaken rock,
because the eye that never sleeps sees everything.

3. Joseph's body was held in bondage, but the chaste champion
   kept his mind and will free.
   He, who once dreamed he was a king, had now been sold as a slave.
   Nevertheless, the captive controlled his captors.
By his master he was praised; by his mistress he was desired.
   The master's intentions were honorable;
   the mistress' obsessions were futile.

High-minded Potiphar genuinely admired Joseph;
>   his base wife tried to bewitch her noble slave.
Joseph's upright behavior delighted his master;
>   Joseph's handsome face tortured his mistress.
The husband entrusted his household to Joseph;
>   the shameless wife surrendered her body to his.
When Joseph realized this, he fled,
>   knowing that a terrible judgment awaits the sinner,
because the eye that never sleeps sees everything.

4. In these scandalous circumstances, the natural order
>   was totally reversed: a slave governed his passions;
>   he was the perfect master of any pleasure.
>   His mistress became a war-captive of sins.
All sinners are slaves of passion:
>   they regard every other action a dream,
>   as they are drawn toward the objects of their desires.
This is exactly what happened to Potiphar's wife,
>   magnetized by lust for her handsome slave.
As she darted at the youth with trembling eyes,
>   her judgement was shattered by invisible blows.
The more his beauty gleamed,
>   the more her mind was dazzled.
In her hand burned a torch of heedless pleasure;
>   in his hand, the unquenchable beacon of purity,
because the eye that never sleeps sees everything.

5. The mania of desire totally gripped the heart of the Egyptian woman.
>   She was stunned by a phantom stroke;
>   bitter poison flooded the wound—
>   but in her frenzy every slash was sweet.
Arrows shot by the steadfast archer penetrated her eyes.
>   The wretched woman dug at her throbbing lust,
>   but the piercing pain was ecstasy.
Rampaging desire laid siege to her mind,
>   but she could not reveal her passion.
When Joseph was present, she burned in agony;
>   when he left, the flames blazed even higher.
In her eagerness to tempt and overcome him,

she enticed him with marvelous invitations.
but pure Joseph parried
    the forbidden thrusts of his mistress,
because the eye that never sleeps sees everything.

6. The devil came to bolster the Egyptian woman,
    he would escort the adulterous bride:
    "Be hard. Use yourself as a hook, tempered and tested.
    Prepare the bait, land the youth," he said.
"Braid the locks of your hair into a snare for him.
    Adorn your face with cosmetics:
    scarlet lips, beguiling eyes.
Coil chains of gleaming gold around your neck;
    drape your body in precious silks.
Apply your most potent perfumes—they soften any young man—
    for the struggle will be titanic and Olympic.
You must attack with lust.
    He will defend himself with purity.
You must not be defeated; we cannot be mocked.
    For he is sure to say, 'I will not do what you desire,
because the eye that never sleeps sees everything.'"

7. When she flaunted her pollutions before the chaste youth,
    he loathed what he saw. The display was magnificent,
    but he recognized the twisted motives behind the splendor
    and rushed to flee from temptation, as from a lurking serpent.
Now the miserable woman could not endure the prudent hero's scorn.
    She ripped away the last shame from her breast
    and exposed her naked lust.
At first, she approached and soothed him through a confidante;
    then she herself summoned him time after time to chat.
Her tongue was sharper than a scimitar,
    able to kill with honey-sweet words.
She tried to bewitch him with every wile,
    but she did not pervert his mind and will.
For he replied, "I shall not do this abomination.
    I have always despised what is squalid,
because the eye that never sleeps sees everything."

8. The maniacal abandon of the profligate woman
   was utterly rebuffed by Joseph.
   When she saw that he was not yielding to her flattery,
   not surrendering to the hot passions of youth, she screamed:
"I bought you as my slave. You were sold to me to serve me.
   I have made you the master of the entire household.
   Now become the master of your mistress.
I do not consider it an insult to lower myself before you,
   since there is no real difference between master and slave.
I have been taught that one man, Adam, is the father of all men
   and that one woman, Eve, is our primeval mother.
All men have been created equal,
   since we all share the same human nature.
Do not fear that you are committing some terrible offense.
   Do not believe those who try to tell you
that the eye that never sleeps sees everything.

9. "Since I see that your behavior is perfect in every regard,
   I honor you above all your fellow slaves.
   In your eyes, complete respect; on your lips, total obedience.
   You are very sensitive to my moods, just as I desire.
Come close, listen to me; I shall make my proposition clear.
   If you yield to me, I shall heap upon you unimaginable riches,
   return your favors with magnificent rewards.
I would recommend you even more highly to my husband,
   and do everything to see that you are immediately freed.
Look, the man who sleeps with his mistress cannot be called a slave.
   But, if you do not yield to me, you will pay a just penalty.
I shall turn you over to barbed shackles.
   I shall hand you over to a painful death.
Do not choose this unnecessary punishment.
   Your beliefs are absurd. It is not true
that the eye that never sleeps sees everything."

10. That was like what the woman said, but she was utterly unable
    to shake the unassailable bastion: Joseph was not lulled
    to sleep by her cooing. He held his judgement on quick alert
    and guarded the untarnished pride of his purity.

Everywhere he patrolled, he spied his frenzied mistress.
    She had dismissed everyone else from the palace.
    It had come to single combat. She shouted:
"How long must I endure your insolence?
    Now is the moment for me to revel in the bed I have desired.
There is absolutely no one in the palace.
    Nothing can prevent my words from becoming deeds."
She flung these spears of fire down at him,
    but she did not ignite his passion.
For from his heart he poured forth streams of self-control
    to smother her lewd intimacies,
because the eye that never sleeps sees everything.

11. As the rabid woman was ranting and straining
    to seduce her young slave Joseph,
        this Olympic athlete stepped into the arena of the ultimate test.
    He would grapple his slippery opponent to the sand.
A pair of seconds entered, each at the side of her favorite:
    Chastity stood at Joseph's shoulder;
    Lewdness bolstered the woman's challenge.
The champion of purity moved to the center of the arena;
    the wily woman circled toward him.
She whispered the delights of adultery;
    the heroic youth coiled to crush the shameless woman.
Angels mustered to support Joseph;
    devils marched with Potiphar's wife.
In the heavens, the Lord observed the struggle
    and crowned his victor with odes of triumph,
because the eye that never sleeps sees everything.

12. Joseph countered the raving woman's challenge
    with words of chaste denial:
        "I am your slave, sold as the unjust victim of jealousy.
    My body was purchased; my will is free.
Paper and ink cannot blot out nobility of character,
    any more than mist which shrouds the sky
    can dim the splendor of the sun.

When clouds are scattered by pursuing winds,
then the sun's rays gleam in glory.
Just so, my slavery will pass away
and my freedom will shine again.
All the land of Egypt will serve me,
because I did not serve your disgusting pleasure.
Long ago he gave me that prophecy—
he who alone foresees the future,
because the eye that never sleeps sees everything.

13. When she heard Joseph's reply,
Potiphar's wife tried to flatter him again and said:
"You never adopted the character of a slave.
I learned that from your actions: of that I am certain.
You have discharged your duties in a way fitting for a free man.
In every task your performance has been flawless,
and you have brought no harm to your fellow-slaves.
So, you are obviously the offspring of noble parents.
This is the reason you have come into my hands,
so that I can become the source of magnificent riches for you,
so that through me the land of Egypt will serve you.
One condition though: I am your mistress,
who harbors great love for you—
take me now into shared ecstasy,
do not be frightened, stop worrying
that the eye that never sleeps sees everything."

14. After these desperate pleas, Joseph replied
to that utterly wanton woman:
"What you say is true. I am a branch of a noble vine.
But you are irrational; I flee any connection with you.
For, whenever someone loses reason as the reins of his life,
he bolts like a senseless beast
and flings himself into forbidden pleasure.
That is why I do not submit to passion, to the joys of the flesh.
I curb their spasms with control of steel.
In the past I have been pure of such pollution;
now I am not going to foul my body with adultery.

30

It is a grave sin to desecrate
    the marriage of another man.
It is, I judge, an even greater crime
    to violate the bed of my master,
because the eye that never sleeps sees everything."

15. "Now listen to me, young man," replied Potiphar's wife
    to the champion of self-control.
    "You know well, your master obeys my desires in every instance.
    I can ruin you or place you at his right hand.
From his past impressions, he has great expectations of you,
    and he cherishes me as his totally chaste wife.
    Until now I have been beyond reproach.
As I have said, since the master trusts us,
    and since no one on earth can see what we do,
why do you balk at obeying your mistress' invitation?
    This is an opportunity which *your* pleas could never have won.
The walls hide us on every side;
    the roof is firmly fixed above us.
Have no fear where there is no fear.
    Do not be frightened. Stop imagining
that the eye that never sleeps sees everything."

16. Striving to bring the wretched woman to her senses,
    chaste Joseph replied:
    "Do not advise me to do evil, as Eve once tempted Adam. Stop!
    I shall not taste that tree which makes death my companion.
Purity is my paradise—it blossoms with every fragrance.
    What is more marvelous than purity?
    Those who faithfully cultivate it shine like angels.
Even if the members of the household do not see our sin
    because humans cannot see what is hidden,
my conscience will sit in accusation
    if I dare to perform this illicit deed.
Even if no one will expose my adultery,
    I have a judge who needs no indictment.
I shudder when I think of him,
    and I flee from forbidden pleasures,
because the eye that never sleeps sees everything.

17. "Suppose I believe you that the walls will hide us on all sides
    when we violate the law and that no one on earth
    can see the sins you desire to commit with me—
    tell me this, woman, where will we flee the one who sees every secret?
Your husband is not present, but my judge is never absent.
    And even if the lord of your bed cannot see me,
    The Lord who judges every secret shall see me.
How can I deceive him who examines our innermost hearts?
    The sky itself will be stirred against me.
It is foolish to rely on walls which offer no protection;
    the roof of heaven cannot cover adultery:
everything is naked and obvious
    to him who knows our hidden sins.
So, I cannot endure to commit
    what is evil in the sight of the Lord,
because the eye that never sleeps sees everything.

18. Inflamed by these arguments, the maddened woman
    rushed at the chaste young man.
    She grabbed his tunic, violently clutched her pure slave:
    "Listen to me, my beloved. Come, make love with me."
Potiphar's wife dragged him down: divine Grace pulled him back.
    "Sleep with me," the Egyptian gasped.
    Heavenly Grace countered, "Stay awake with me."
At the mistress' side the devil struggled bitterly,
    locking the valiant athlete in his mighty grasp.
The angel of purity moved into the arena again
    and strained to break their hold.
"Tear away his tunic," the angel commanded,
    "but dare not violate his pure body.
For from the hands of this contest's heavenly judge,
    Joseph, the victor, will receive the robe of uncorruptibility,
because the eye that never sleeps sees everything.

19. Because he fought so valiantly for his chastity,
    Joseph won the hero's wreath. To guard the treasure
    of his purity, the youth stripped off his tunic;
    but, crowned victor, he donned robes of incontestable glory.

The Egyptian lunged, like the fabled fox pawing a grape vine.
Each hoped to snatch the entire cluster;
both were left with a handful of leaves.
In Heaven the angels rejoiced with righteous Joseph:
in Hell the demons wailed with the lawless woman.
The prudent youth threw aside his outer garment
to keep his inner life unstained.
The brazen woman wrapped herself in a cloak of madness,
after letting fall all sense of shame.
Wise Joseph is honored as he deserves
for fleeing the gravest of sins,
because the eye that never sleeps sees everything.

20. What hymn can I sing worthy of such a celebrated hero?
His deeds surpass all praise.
Like a taut ship he sailed away from savage storms of lust
and dropped anchor in chastity's calm harbor.
He trampled out the coals of passion blazing in the palace.
Drawing draughts of heavenly dew,
he smothered the ravenous force of the flame.
That was the titanic contest of glorious Joseph,
and this is my victory ode for that noble athlete.
What was done then in the hidden recesses of the palace
is praised in song each day throughout the universe.
For noble character is never engulfed
by the tidal wave of temptation.
The Redeemer rescues his faithful servants
from the floods of sin,
because the eye that never sleeps sees everything.

21. Long ago Joseph's brothers plotted against him
because they envied his royal dreams.
Eager to destroy him, they devised an elaborate scheme,
which fell just short of accursed murder:
they dipped his robe in blood, but did not strike the one who wore it.
God guarded Joseph's life
while Jacob mourned his death.

Later, the Egyptian adulteress also attacked his fortress-robe,
    but she could not wound the soul of the heroic warrior.
For Joseph was clad in inviolable armor
    which deflected all the missiles of her passion.
My faithful brothers, let us strive to imitate this champion,
    because even today
lust of the flesh marches against us.
    Yet no one will be defeated by temptation,
because the eye that never sleeps sees everything.

22. The Olympic master of his passion has earned
    a heavenly crown and a victory ode.
We Christians, always and everywhere, rightfully honor
    his memory, because sin did not enslave his body.
When the lewd woman wheedled him with word and deed,
    Joseph spurned her shameless promises.
He chose death rather than the dungeon of lust.
What shall I, your Melodist, do in my own misery and guilt,
    since sin always clutches me in her hand?
Just as Potiphar's wife once assaulted Joseph,
    so too does temptation drag me toward forbidden desires.
But I cry to you, omnipotent Lord:
    "Christ, ransom me from the tyranny of sin
so that, aided by the Virgin Mother of God,
    I may prove as faithful a servant as Joseph was,
because the eye that never sleeps sees everything."

Translated from the Greek by R. J. Schork

THE AKATHISTOS HYMN, thought to be written sometime in the 5th or 6th centuries, is a Byzantine Greek hymn to the Virgin Mary, which has become an important part of the Greek Orthodox liturgy.

I. When he grasped the command secretly entrusted to him,
    he rushed to the dwelling of Joseph;
        there the incorporeal messenger said to the inviolable Virgin:
"The Lord who bends the heavens in his descent
    comes to dwell wholly in you, without any change.
As I see him taking the shape of a servant in your womb,
    I stand back in awe and salute you,
'Hail, unwedded bride!'"

[II. Mother of God, Constantinople chants its thanks to you
    in a victory paean. You are my champion, my commander.
    You have rescued me from the terrors of the siege.
Now, since you possess unassailable power,
    free me from every sort of peril,
        so that I can cry out to you:
"Hail, unwedded bride!"

III. Mother of God, it is totally right for us not to cease
our hymns of praise to you, as we sing,
"Hail, unwedded bride!"]

1. An angel from the highest rank in heaven was sent
    to proclaim the Mother of God with "Hail!"
And as he uttered that incorporeal sound
    the messenger saw that you were made flesh, Lord.
He drew back, at attention, singing such salutations to the Virgin:
    "Hail, because of you joyous grace will shine forth.
Hail, for you altars of sacrifice will be left behind.
    Hail, restoration of the fall of Adam.

35

Hail, cessation of the tears of Eve.

    Hail, height unapproachable to human minds.

Hail, depth unfathomable even to angelic eyes.

    Hail, you are the throne of our King.

Hail, you carry him who holds the universe.

    Hail, star which lights the sun.

Hail, womb of the divine incarnation.

    Hail, through you all creation is generated anew.

Hail, through you the Creator is worshiped.

    Hail, unwedded bride!"

2. **Boldly** the Virgin replied to the Archangel Gabriel,

    since the Blessed One knew her purity was intact:

"The paradox of your declaration

    seems incomprehensible to my mind.

You announce a conception without seed, and cry 'Alleluia.'"

3. **Groping** to grasp this concept, the Virgin sought light

    and spoke with force to God's minister:

"How is it possible for a son to be born

    from immaculate loins? Tell me that."

The archangel replied in fear, but his words were jubilant:

    "Hail, vestal handmaiden of the ineffable will.

Hail, willing devotee of silence-shrouded faith.

    Hail, prelude to the miraculous works of Christ.

Hail, compendium of the teachings of the Lord.

    Hail, celestial ladder on which God descends.

Hail, bridge leading those from earth to Heaven.

    Hail, incessantly chanted wonder of the angels.

Hail, unceasingly lamented wound of the demons.

    Hail, mysterious deliverer of the Light.

Hail, consternation of those who ask 'How?'

    Hail, understanding greater than the knowledge of the wise.

Hail, belief illuminating the minds of the faithful.

    Hail, unwedded bride!"

4. Dynamic shadows of the All-high then rippled
   over the Virgin, and she was with child.
With a fine brush God wished to portray her fertile womb
   as a lush field prepared for all who wish
to reap the harvest of salvation by chanting "Alleluia!"

5. Encompassing God in her womb, the Virgin
   rushed to visit Elizabeth.
Her cousin's child immediately recognized
Mary's unsown seedling and rejoiced.
His womb-leaps were hosannas to the Mother of God:
"Hail, shoot from a bud that will never wither.
   Hail, vintage from an unadulterated cluster.
Hail, field bearing the Cultivator of our race.
   Hail, garden producing the Source of our life.
Hail, plowland flourishing with the Relief of our miseries.
   Hail, mesa land teeming with Thanks-offerings.
Hail, you make the meadows blossom with delight.
   Hail, you make ready a harbor for our souls.
Hail, incense-altar wreathed in prayers.
   Hail, propitiation of the entire world.
Hail, bond between God and mortals.
   Hail, entente between mortals and God.
   Hail, unwedded bride!"

6. Zeal for the Virgin's reputation, worry about her state—
   these conflicts stormed in the mind of prudent Joseph.
He gazed at you in wonder, his betrothed one,
   and he imagined you betrayed his trust, blameless one.
But when he learned you conceived by the Holy Spirit, he said "Alleluia!"

7. Hearing the hymn of the angels, the shepherds
   knew that Christ's incarnation was a reality.
They ran to him as to the High Shepherd,
   and they beheld him like a flawless lamb
cradled in the bosom of Mary. This was their hymn:
"Hail, Mother of the Lamb and the Shepherd.
   Hail, fold open to all the human flock.

Hail, protection against invisible beasts.
    Hail, woman who unlocked the gates of Paradise.
Hail, because heaven and earth reconciled.
    Hail, because creatures of clay dance with loyal angels.
Hail, silent voice of all God's messengers.
    Hail, invincible courage of all God's champions.
Hail, unshaken pillar of our faith.
    Hail, undimmed beacon of our charity.
Hail, because of you Hell has been stripped naked.
    Hail, because of you we clothe ourselves in glory.
    Hail, unwedded bride!"

8. The Magi saw that the star was God's pathfinder
    and they followed the road of its rays.
They regarded Christ as their shining light;
    they searched for him as for a powerful king.
Then, beholding the One who cannot be grasped, they cried "Alleluia!"

9. In the arms of the Virgin, the princes of the Chaldeans
    saw the Being who molded mortals in his hands.
They recognized him as their Master—
    even in the form of a slave—and were eager
to honor him with gifts and salute his Holy Mother:
"Hail, Mother of the Star that never sets.
    Hail, dawn of the mystic day.
Hail, you shut down the forge of deception.
    Hail, you protect those who serve the Trinity.
Hail, you have cast the unhuman tyrant from power.
    Hail, you reveal Christ as the Lord loving all humans.
Hail, you who are freed from barbarian worship.
    Hail, you who are untouched by the slime of magic.
Hail, you who extinguished the adoration of idol-fire.
    Hail, you who deflected the flames of lust.
Hail, you lead the pagan Persians on the path of purity.
    Hail, you are the jubilation of every nation.
    Hail, unwedded bride!"

10. Kingly messengers of God's Word, the Magi
    returned to Babylon, Lord;
they spread your oracular gospel far to the East
    an announced to all that you are the Messiah.
They dismissed Herod as a fool too ignorant to sing "Alleluia!"

11. Light of truth began to shine even in Egypt
    as you dispersed the darkness of falsehood.
Lord, you cast down the idols of that land—
    they could not match your might.
Those delivered from pagan power cried to God's Mother:
"Hail, restoration of the human race.
    Hail, demolition of the hellish horde.
Hail, you have trampled down the errors of deception.
    Hail, you have exposed the fraud of idolatry.
Hail, sea that submerged the fantasies of the Pharaohs.
    Hail, rock that satisfied those who thirst for truth.
Hail, pillar of fire that guides those in darkness.
    Hail, refuge of the world, broader than any cloud.
Hail, food more nourishing than manna.
    Hail, purveyor of hallowed delight.
Hail, land of God's promise.
    Hail, land flowing with milk and honey.
    Hail, unwedded bride!"

12. Meager time in this fleeting world of deception
    was left for the Prophet Simeon
when you were presented to him as an infant, Lord;
    but he immediately recognized God in all perfection.
Awestruck at your infinite wisdom, he exclaimed "Alleluia!"

13. Now the Creator has appeared and has revealed
    a new creation to us who were formed by him:
this child has sprung from womb without seed,
    and he guards that womb, perpetually inviolate.
As we behold this wonder, let us raise a hymn to Mary:
"Hail, flower of incorruptibility.
    Hail, garland of chastity.

Hail, light foreshadowing the resurrection.
Hail, revelation of angelic life.
Hail, tree with gleaming fruit that feeds the faithful.
Hail, trunk shrouded by lush leaves that shelter all.
Hail, carrier of the Saviour who ransoms sin's captives.
Hail, bearer of the Guide who directs the lost.
Hail, intercession before the Just Judge.
Hail, contrition in the face of countless faults.
Hail, mantle of open generosity for the naked.
Hail, pure love vanquishing any lust.
Hail, unwedded bride!

14. Exclude the world, embrace Heaven with our hearts,
my comrades, since we have seen this marvelous child.
This is the reason why the Most High has appeared
on earth as a humble human being.
He wished to raise to the heights those who shout "Alleluia!"

15. On the plains of earth as in the plateaus of Heaven,
the uncircumscribed Word of God is totally present.
The simultaneity of his presence is a divine attribute,
not some material exchange of place.
He is the child of the divinely chosen Virgin, to whom we say,
"Hail, homeland of the boundless God.
Hail, gateway of the hallowed liturgy.
Hail, reverberation numbing the infidels.
Hail, ringing proclamation of the faithful.
Hail, all-holy chariot of him whom the cherubim support.
Hail, perfect shelter of him whom the seraphim house.
Hail, woman in whom all opposites are reconciled.
Hail, woman who joins virginity and childbirth.
Hail, woman through whom sin was erased.
Hail, woman through whom Paradise was reopened.
Hail, key to the kingdom of Christ.
Hail, hope of eternal happiness.
Hail, unwedded bride!"

16. **P**andemonium struck the angelic ranks when they heard
   of the Virgin's role in the incarnation.
For they witnessed the unapproachable being of God
   become a human creature approachable to all.
He dwells in our midst and hears on every side "Alleluia!"

17. **R**hetoricians with silver tongues become mute as fish
   in your presence, Mother of God.
They are at a loss to explain how you remain
   a virgin yet were able to give birth.
We too are amazed at this mystery, but we loyally chant:
"Hail, ark of the wisdom of God.
   Hail, treasury of God's foreknowledge.
Hail, woman who reveals the foolishness of the learned.
   Hail, woman who exposes the inanities of science.
Hail, you reduced awesome advocates to a pack of idiots.
   Hail, you banished creators of poetic nonsense.
Hail, you sever the skeins of Greek logic choppers.
   Hail, you fill the seines of Christ's fishers of men.
Hail, you drag us out of the abyss of ignorance.
   Hail, you enlighten many with knowledge.
Hail. ship transporting those who want to be saved.
   Hail, harbor of those who have finished life's voyage.
Hail, unwedded bride!"

18. **S**ince he wished to save his creatures, the world's Creator,
   entirely of his own will, came into the world.
Our God appeared as a shepherd for us;
   for us he became a creature like us.
While he calls like to like, as God he hears "Alleluia!"

19. **T**rue bastion of all virgins, Virgin Mother of God,
   you protect everyone who comes to you.
The Creator of heaven and earth,
   made you ready, undefiled Mary.
He dwelled in your womb and taught all to cry out to you:
"Hail, column of virginity.
   Hail, gate of salvation.

Hail, chief guide of unwavering understanding.
    Hail, supplier of divine goodness.
Hail, you regenerate those conceived in shame.
    Hail, you stabilize those whose minds totter.
Hail, you nullify elements which corrupt our senses.
    Hail, you gave birth to the sower of chastity.
Hail, bridal chamber of a wedding without union.
    Hail, you link all the faithful to the Lord.
Hail, noble, Son-bearing paragon of virgins.
    Hail, bridesmaid of all sanctified souls.
    Hail, unwedded bride!"

20. Under the onslaught of litanies chanted by those
    who beg your mercy, any other hymn fades away.
Even if we direct to you psalms balanced
    by an equal number of odes, Hallowed King,
we would not match what has been given to us who sing "Alleluia!"

21. **Ph**osphorescent rays penetrate the world's darkness:
    we behold our Lamp, the Holy Virgin.
For, just as she kindled the immaterial Light,
    so she guides everyone to God-like understanding.
Her beams illumine the mind; she deserves our hymn:
"Hail, radiation from the spiritual Sun.
    Hail, splendor from the unsetting Light.
Hail, lightning stroke coruscating over our souls.
    Hail, thunderclap confounding our foes.
Hail, you lift the candelabra with countless flames.
    Hail, you unleash the river with infinite currents.
Hail, you drew a perfect model of the baptismal fount.
    Hail, you took away the stain of sin.
Hail, sponge that wipes our consciences clean.
    Hail, krater in which our eternal joy is blended.
Hail, essence of the perfume of Christ.
    Hail, life-source of the mystical banquet.
    Hail, unwedded bride!"

22. **Ch**rist wished his grace to abolish our primeval debts,
  for he can cancel the lien on the human race.
The Lord gave himself to bring back to his house
  those who had strayed far from his favor.
He tore up sin's mortgage and hears all of us singing "Alleluia!"

23. **Ps**alms to your Son and shouts of praise from all of us to you,
  Mother of God; he is a living temple.
While he dwelled in your womb,
  the Lord held the universe in his hand;
he sanctified and glorified you, taught us all to sing:
"Hail, tabernacle of God and the Word.
  Hail, shrine more hallowed than the Holy of Holies.
Hail, ark filled with gold by the Holy Spirit.
  Hail, undepleted treasury of life.
Hail, blesser of the precious diadem of the emperors.
  Hail, guarantor of the august glory of the priests.
Hail, unassailable tower of the Church.
  Hail, unviolable rampart of the empire.
Hail, Virgin by whom victory trophies are built.
  Hail, Virgin by whom our enemies are scattered.
Hail, loyal patron of our mortal flesh.
  Hail, royal court of our immortal souls.
  Hail, unwedded bride!"

24. **O** Mother praised in every hymn, you gave birth
  to the Word who dwells in every Holy of Holies.
Receive this offering of our song,
  rescue each of us from every misfortune,
and save from punishment to come those who cry to you "Alleluia!"

Translated from the Greek by R.J. Schork

St. Yared (505-571) was an Ethiopian hymn writer, composer and priest. He was born in the village of Axum in the Axumite Kingdom. He spent much of his life as an itinerant teacher. Eventually, he settled in the Semien Mountains, where he continued to compose and teach until his death.

FROM *THE ASSUMPTION OF MARY*

There, in Abraham's burial plot,
    sister of him who brought
        down the law, whose father fought
            the giant, shines the pearl long sought,
                where, in her clothing's herbal-scented knot,
            he is caught.
The honoured star
    whose light is spread out far
        over the earth; her deeds are,
            yes, they are,
                known in Lydda's square.
To George, who's buried there,
dear lady, send your prayer
that he should make our foes despair.

Purest bridal room,
    liberator, in whom
        divinity came to be enwombed.
            She wears his glory as fit costume,
                who is also Moses' burning broom.
Holy of holies is your name,
for always have your lips declaimed
pure honey, O most blessed dame.

Treasure chest where God interred
   his everlasting word;
      halo that begirds
         the moon; heat transferred
            from the sun; your fruit, deferred
               to the belly, makes wisdom heard;
                  flaming tree which has the understanding stirred.
Heaven names her as his dove,
since she is paragon of
silence, humility and love.

The Lord of all was swayed
   by the beauty of this maid,
      daughter of light arrayed
         to be salvation's aid.
            She was the bridal arcade
               where Jesus' grandeur was displayed,
                  the gate that glory to men conveyed.
Mary, great bearer of the light,
hear our terrible plight.
   New calf, it is you we praise;
   angels name you, for the rest of days,
   dear sister to the human race.

Mary, whom they call upright,
   virginity so bright
      corruption cannot blight
         such wool of purest white,
            or cloud of clearest light,
               ringed by seraphim in flight.
O dear Mary, hear our plea
that his kingdom we might see
when his coming he decrees.
   Let him have us stand before him;
   Let him call us to adore him;
   Jesus Christ eternal lord then.

From *The Finding of the True Cross*

Look and proclaim, how good
it is that men have obtained
this exalted wood.
Brief gold was not the currency
    to purchase back man's soul,
        but with his precious blood
            he chose to pay that toll.
The cross shines out.
The cross shines out and is so bright
that earthly kings do trail its light;
the thing that seemed so dark and damp
is now the world's great guiding lamp.
The cross's feast takes place
    both high in heaven's face
and low upon the earth.
    We know its worth,
prize and praise it, with no dearth
    of trust. It is man's rebirth
and help in need.

Translated from the Ge'ez by Burl Horniachek with Ralph Lee

St. Venantius Fortunatus (c. 530–600/609) was a Frankish bishop, poet and hymn writer. He was born at Duplavis (present-day Valdobbiadene) in north-eastern Italy. He spent most of his life in the Merovingian capital of Metz, in what is present-day north-eastern France.

Sing, My Tongue, the Saviour's Glory

Sing, my tongue, the Saviour's glory;
Tell His triumph far and wide;
Tell aloud the famous story
Of His body crucified;
How upon the cross a victim,
Vanquishing in death, He died.

Eating of the tree forbidden,
Man had sunk in Satan's snare,
When our pitying Creator did
This second tree prepare;
Destined, many ages later,
That first evil to repair.

Such the order God appointed
When for sin He would atone;
To the serpent thus opposing
Schemes yet deeper than his own;
Thence the remedy procuring,
Whence the fatal wound had come.

So when now at length the fullness
of the sacred time drew nigh,
Then the Son, the world's Creator,
Left his Father's throne on high;
From a virgin's womb appearing,
Clothed in our mortality.

All within a lowly manger,
Lo, a tender babe He lies!
See his gentle Virgin Mother
Lull to sleep his infant cries!
While the limbs of God incarnate
'Round with swathing bands she ties.

Thus did Christ to perfect manhood
In our mortal flesh attain:
Then of His free choice He goeth
To a death of bitter pain;
And as a lamb, upon the altar of the cross,
For us is slain.

Lo, with gall His thirst He quenches!
See the thorns upon His brow!
Nails His tender flesh are rending!
See His side is opened now!
Whence, to cleanse the whole creation,
Streams of blood and water flow.

Faithful Cross! Above all other,
One and only noble Tree!
None in foliage, none in blossom,
None in fruit thy peers may be;
Sweetest wood and sweetest iron!
Sweetest Weight is hung on thee!

Lofty tree, bend down thy branches,
To embrace thy sacred load;
Oh, relax the native tension
Of that all too rigid wood;
Gently, gently bear the members
Of thy dying King and God.

Tree, which solely wast found worthy
The world's Victim to sustain.
Harbor from the raging tempest!
Ark, that saved the world again!
Tree, with sacred blood anointed
Of the Lamb for sinners slain.

Blessing, honor, everlasting,
To the immortal Deity;
To the Father, Son, and Spirit,
Equal praises ever be;
Glory through the earth and heaven
To Trinity in Unity. Amen.

Translated from the Latin by Edward Caswall

ST. JOHN OF DAMASCUS (c. 675–749) was a Byzantine Greek monk, priest, theologian and poet. He was born and raised in Damascus, but lived most of his life in monasteries near Jerusalem. As a theologian, he is especially known for his vigourous defense of icons and as a precursor to Scholasticism.

PASCHAL CANON

α

The day of resurrection, may all God's people brim
    with light. The Lord's Passover!
From out of death to life, from Earth to heaven's rim,
    we're borne by the Prime Mover
our God Christ, as we sing out his victory hymn.

May all our senses be perfected; may we see,
    in resurrection's sheer
untouchable brightness, Christ the Lightning, and may we
    perceive His voice, and hear
His ringing welcome, while we hymn His victory.

Let fitting celebrations exalt the smiling skies;
    let raptures seize the earth.
Let all the seen and unseen cosmos melt in cries
    of universal mirth.
The transport of the ages, Christ, awakes to rise.

γ

    We quaff a drink unknown, untried,
not coaxed from a sterile stone by wizardry,
but the immortal source
    that from the tomb of Christ like rainfall pours,
    by which we're made and fortified.

Light charges all things far and wide:
the earth, the world beneath it, and the sky;
now all Creation quakes
with merriment and joy as Christ awakes,
    in whom we're made and fortified.

Christ, yesterday I was in the tomb
with you; today, you rise, and so do I.
Yesterday, we two
were crucified; now, Savior, make me new
    within your glorious kingdom come.

δ
Where Habbakuk stands watch, the mouthpiece of God's throne,
    let us stand and be shown
the angel, with torch flaming,
powerfully proclaiming,
    "This is the world's deliverance,
for Christ is risen in omnipotence!"

Christ appeared and opened the Virgin's womb as "male,"
    this "human," whom we hail
as Lamb; our Paschal Feast,
who has not lipped the least
    of sins, we call Wholly Unflawed;
we call Him perfect, as He is true God.

Like to a yearling lamb, crown of our blessings, Christ
    gladly is sacrificed,
a Passover to cleanse
all people of our sins;
    in good time rising from death's door,
the Sun of Justice beams on us once more.

God's forefather, David, danced joyful by the ark,
   though he was half in dark.
May we, God's people, seeing
God's full intention being
   fulfilled, be roused by God to dance,
for Christ is risen in omnipotence.

ε

   Awaking in the dead
pre-dawn, we'll meet the Lord with music's balm, not myrrh's,
and see the Sun of Justice, Christ, as he climbs to shed
   light and life on the universe.

   Great crowds, whom Satan's fetters
once bound, behold the boundlessness of your compassion,
and surge to the light, o Christ; their steps' quick gladness clatters
   your deathless Passover's ovation.

   With wedding torch in hand,
we'll greet Christ as he quits the grave with a bridegroom's face,
and celebrate, beside a jubilant angel band,
   God's Passover, our saving grace.

ς

Down, down you went, to earth's profoundest vale,
where every iron bar, and each eternal fetter,
   you shattered, Christ; and three days later
you issued from the tomb, like Jonah from the whale.

When you emerged from death, you left in place
the seals of life; the Virgin's locked womb was not torn
   open, Christ, when you were born;
yet you flung open wide the Gates of Paradise.

My Savior, as a sacrifice You gave—
freely to the Father—Yourself, unslain, alive,
   as God, triumphing to revive
Adam's all-fathering seed, in rising from the grave.

ζ
You saved the young men from the furnace,
were born to human peril,
and suffered as a mortal, through suffering to earn us
mortals our fresh, unperishing apparel:
the only God, our fathers' praise,
transcendent now in glory's rays.

Godminded women brought perfume,
taking the path You'd trod;
the mortal whom they sought in tears within the tomb
in joy they worshipped as the living God,
first to proclaim, first to discover,
Christ, your mystical Passover.

The death of Death, Hell's shattered powers,
today win our applause;
the first fruits of the new eternal life that's ours
we celebrate, and dance and sing the Cause:
the only God, our fathers' praise,
transcendent now in glory's rays.

How worthy of our feast of honor,
how truly holy, this
night of sunshine and salvation, this forerunner
of resurrection's brilliant day of bliss,
when, freed from time and burial,
embodied light beamed on us all.

η
This is the holy Day of Days ordained for men,
the First of Sabbaths, Queen and Sovereign,
the Feast of Feasts, the Jubilee of Jubilees,
in which we glorify Christ to the centuries.

This day of resurrection, let's taste what we are given:
     the new fruit of the vine, the joy of heaven,
the kingdom of Christ come—this signal day of praise!—
while we hymn Christ as God unto the end of days.

Sion, lift up your eyes and look about: be awed.
     Behold, your sons have come like flares from God
out of the West and North, from Dawn and from the seas,
as they bless Christ in you unto the centuries.

O Father of all power, of life the Word and Wind,
     one Nature where Three Persons interblend,
Thou past Godhead and Being, baptized in You we raise
all adoration always, unto the end of days.

θ
     O new Jerusalem, shine now, shine bright!
The glory of the Lord has beamed on you, and smiled.
     O Sion, dance in your delight!
     And you, rejoice, God's Mother, undefiled,
     at the arising of your Child.

     Voice of surpassing sweetness we adore!
O holy voice that truly swore You, Christ, would be
     with us until time is no more!
     This is the anchor of our hope which we,
     the faithful, grasp rejoicingly.

     O great Passover, incorruptible,
o Christ, who are God's word, His wisdom, and His might,
     grant that we, too, may taste the full
     grace of Your presence in the broad daylight
     of your empire that knows no night.

                    Translated from the Greek by Christopher Childers

St. Cosmas of Maiouma (d. 773 or 794) was a Byzantine Greek priest, monk and poet. He was probably born in Damascus, but was orphaned and then adopted by the father of St. John of Damascus. The two brothers lived together in monasteries near Jerusalem, until Cosmas was appointed Bishop of Maiouma in Gaza in 743.

Canon for Holy Saturday Matins

Acrostic: TODAY I SING THE GREAT HIGH HOLY SABBATH

α
The children of the saved have buried in the grave
    the One who, in old days,
buried pursuing Pharaoh under an ocean wave;
now let us, like the maidens, make the hymn we raise:
    How glorious is Thy praise!

O Lord, my God, I shall pour out with my full breath
    a dirge-song, a death-knell,
and hymn of Exodus: for You have, by Your death,
opened the paths of life; and by your burial
    dealt death to Death and Hell.

Descrying You entombed below, enthroned on high,
    the heights of the universe
and depths beneath the earth, my Savior, were struck by
your death and trembled; past conceiving, Lord, your corse
    emerged as life's prime source.

All the way down you went, o Friend of Man, and sought
    earth's bottom, to imbue
the whole with glory. Adam's self in me was not
hidden from your view. Entombed, Beloved, You
    make me, corrupted, new.

γ
You, who hung the whole of Earth upon the sea
              unconstrainably
hung upon Calvary, where all Creation saw
    thunderstruck, and cried in awe:
                              No one
       is holy, Lord, but You alone.

Images and symbols of the coming passion
              You poured forth in profusion.
In hell, Your godmanship shot light, illumining
    Your hidden depths. All cried: "My King!
                              None, none
       is holy, Lord, but You alone."

Spheres which had been sundered You have unified
    with Your embrace flung wide.
O Savior, in your vault and in your linen shroud
    you freed the chained, who cried aloud:
    No one
    is holy, Lord, but You alone.

Inside your stone-sealed tomb, unbudgeable, You stayed
    true to Your will, unswayed.
Your godly deeds make real, for us, Your potency,
    who sing, "Friend of Humanity!
    None, none
    is holy, Lord, but You alone."

δ
Nailed Cross-wise, emptying to God,
You stunned presageful Habakkuk, who shouted, awed:
"All goodness, You've lopped off the head of every prince
    and warred down Hell in Your omnipotence."

God's holy seventh day—You blessed it
today, as You did when, Your work complete, You rested.
All that You made then, now You've made new, and restored,
    and keep Your Sabbath still, Redeemer Lord.

The sinew of supreme control
gave You the victory, at which Your flesh and soul
were parted. By Your power, Word, both parts together
    dissevered Death and Hell's each tie and tether.

Hell, when it met You, met its doom,
o Word: it saw Your corse anointed with perfume,
brindled with weals and welts, and in all acts almighty,
    and perished in the shudder of Your beauty.

ε

Entering in consubstantial
Theophany, o Christ, our human plight,
You showed Isaiah in his pre-dawn vigil
Your never-setting light defeat the night.
"All men shall rise," he cried, "and live again, who died;
    all those upon the earth
and all beneath it shall be full of mirth."

Garbing Yourself in human clay,
You've shaped our earth anew, o Fashioner.
The shroud and sepulcher, Thou Word, convey
the mystery they share with You and are.
The "grandee councilman" advances the grand plan
    of Your great Father, Who,
all Majesty, now makes me new in You.

Rot is reversed by burial;
by dying, You've unravelled death and sin.
God's birthright renders incorruptible
and deifies Your sleeve of mortal skin.
Unmortified, Your flesh remained supremely fresh,
    nor, Lord, did Your soul rest—
strange wayfarer!—for long as Hades' guest.

Exempt, my Maker, from the aching
pangs of labor, still the spearpoint rent
Your side, from whence You fashioned the remaking
of Eve, a second Adam, as you went,
sleeping a sleep past Nature of life for every creature.
      Life, too, You forced awake
from sleep and rot with an Almighty shake.

ς

Abducted, not absorbed, was Jonah's fate
      inside the belly of the whale—
an episode now seen to adumbrate
      Your suffering and burial.
He, stepping from the beast as from a bridal
      chamber, to the guardsmen said:
"You, standing watch for this or that false idol,
      forfeit the mercy you'd have had."

Tortured to death, but not dissociation,
      You saved the flesh You had put on.
For if, upon the instant of Your passion,
      Your holy temple was undone,
still, Word, Your Deity and body share
      a single Substance—for You span
both elements, o Word of God, who Are
      God's only Son, both God and man.

Human death, but not the death of Heaven
      was the upshot of Adam's error.
For though tremendous sufferings had riven
      Your body when You were its bearer,
that suffering left Your Godhead unaffected
      as You, exchanging earthly clay
for incorruption, opened, resurrected,
      a spring of Life beyond decay.

In power, but not in eternal power,
    Hell plies its temporal command.
For You, when You were buried, at that hour
    shattered, with life-creating hand,
the deadbolts of the grave, almighty God,
    and into new, true freedom led
the sleepers there from every period,
    the firstborn Savior of the dead.

ζ

Gift past expressing! He who, in the furnace,
rescued those righteous children from the flame
is laid out dead, devoid of breath, to earn us
    salvation, who in song proclaim,
    O Lord, Redeemer, Savior,
    You are blessed forever!

Hell's heart was speared when it gaped to devour
the One whose side gaped for the soldier's spear;
Hell groans, consumed in Godhead's fire, for our
    salvation, as in song we cheer,
    O Lord, Redeemer, Savior,
    You are blessed forever!

Hallowed tomb! which took unto your breast
the world's Creator, as if slumbering;
now you're the treasure house of life most blessed,
    for our salvation, as we sing:
    O Lord, Redeemer, Savior,
    You are blessed forever!

Omnific life is stretched on the stone floor
of the cold tomb, according to death's law,
to make a spring of resurrection for
    our salvation, who sing in awe:
    O Lord, Redeemer, Savior,
    You are blessed forever!

Linked and indivisible, Christ's Godhead
was triune with the Spirit and the Father
in Hell, in Paradise, and with the dead
    for our salvation, who sing together:
        O Lord, Redeemer, Savior,
        You are blessed forever!
η
You heavens, thrill with awe, and tremble;
foundations of the earth, convulse, disquieted.
The King of all the Heights is numbered with the dead;
    the grave that welcomes Him is humble.
        Servants, sing your praises; Priests, perform your paeans;
        higher than height, o People, lift Him to the aeons.

Stainlessly His temple fell;
that fallen tabernacle is raised up once more.
The King of all the Heights, the second Adam, for
    the first's salvation, harrowed Hell.
        Servants, sing your praises; Priests, perform your paeans;
        higher than height, o People, lift Him to the aeons.

Arimathean Joseph, scrying
the Cross, the Lord of All, His naked form, excelled—
when all of the Disciples lost their nerve, his held.
    That corpse he took and buried, crying
        Servants, sing your praises; Priests, perform your paeans;
        higher than height, o People, lift Him to the aeons.

Benevolence too large for laud!
Forbearance past expressing! Undreamt-of miracle!
The King of Heights is sealed below, of His own will;
    God lets Himself be called a fraud.
        Servants, sing your praises; Priests, perform your paeans;
        higher than height, o People, lift Him to the aeons.

θ

Be far from weeping, Mother, as You see Me in the tomb,
   whom, uninseminated, You carried in Your womb.
   For I shall rise again, to glory and acclaim,
   and shall, as God, commend
   to glory without end
   all who believe, and love, and praise Your name.

Awe-fraught and pangless was the birth with which You hallowed Me,
   o Boy beyond beginning, supernaturally.
   But now I see, my God, that You have really died,
   stabbed by the sword of grief
   I suffer past belief.
   O rise, that my name may be magnified!

The earth takes Me of My own will, but the doormen are distressed
   and shudder by Hell's gate when they behold me dressed,
   dear Mother, in the robes of vengeance, bright with gore.
   With my foes at a loss,
   God-humbled, on the Cross,
   I'll rise again, and praise You evermore.

H*allelujah*! let Creation cry. Let rapture sweeten
   for all Earth's children. Hell, the Enemy, is beaten.
   Let women bearing unguents meet Me on My way
   to rescue Adam, Eve,
   and all they could conceive;
   and I shall rise again on the third day.

Translated from the Greek by Christopher Childers

THE STIKHERA FOR THE LAST KISS is a Byzantine Greek poem which is part of the Greek Orthodox funeral service. It has sometimes been attributed to St. John of Damascus.

Come, O beloveds, come let us give a tender
last kiss to our beloved who has fallen to sleep.

Let us also give thanks to our God,
for even as our friend has left us
and hastens to the grave, he no longer suffers
despair, nor does his flesh suffer distress.

Here where we stand, dear family and friends,
in the midst of this painful parting, pray
that the Lord will give our beloved friend rest.

What manner of parting is this, beloveds?
What manner of mourning pours forth?
What lamentation do we sing at such time?

Come, let us kiss our beloved, who—
short moments ago—stood with us.

As we part from him now, let us pray
he be covered with grace, even as
he is covered with a stone. Residing in darkness
and lain with the dead, may the Lord give deep rest.

Now every evil of vanity suffered through life
is being destroyed, as the spirit departs
from its dwelling. The clay dims into darkness.
The vessel is shattered, falling mute, unfeeling, and still.

As we escort to the grave our beloved, let us pray
that the Lord give him rest for the ages.

What is this life—a flower? a cloud? dew glistening?
Come, therefore, let us look clear-eyed
into the graves. What has become of the beauty,
the body's sweet flesh? And what of its youth?
Where are the eyes? The dear bodily form?
All are withered as grass. All have vanished.

Come, let us fall before Christ in our tears.
This parting of the soul brings great sorrow,
great weeping, heart-rending sighs, deep affliction.

Just as hell and perdition are things passing away,
so the toil of life on earth an untimely illusion
comprised of dim shadow, grim dream within sleep.

Let us flee far from every sinful deed, and thereby
inherit heavenly blessings. Let us look upon
our beloved departed now lying before us.
Let us witness in his departure our own final
moments. He drifts from the earth like smoke.
He is wrapped in a shroud, and delivered to earth.
Even as he lies hidden from sight, let us pray
Christ give him rest now and ever.

May we glimpse in this moment how the soul—
about to be carried off by the fearsome angels—forgets
all that it knows, and becomes mindful only of standing
before the judgement of its folly and fleshly toil.

Come, let us implore the Good Judge, let us pray
that the Lord will pardon every sin committed.

Come, O brethren, let us apprehend in the dust,
in the ashes of the grave, that very dust
from which we were formed, apprehending thereby
where we are going and what we shall become.

What becomes of the poor man? What
of the rich? What becomes of the master and the slave?
Are they not all become ashes? The beauty of every
face turned to dust? The flower of every youth
withered by death? The glories of this life are folly
and corruption. For each will end, and all shall die—
kings and princes, judges and rulers, the rich
and the poor, yea, every kind of mortal man and woman.

For all those committed to the grave, let us pray
that the Lord grant them rest. Every vital element
of the body will grow still. All grow still, fall dead,
without feeling. For the eyes are closed, the feet are bound,
the hands lie motionless, and the ears do not hear.
The tongue is sealed in silence. All elements fail
and are committed to the maw of the grave.

Truly all human efforts are empty, save
those evincing hope in you, O Theotokos,
O mother of the never-setting Sun. Ask Him
Who is exceedingly good that He will grant
to this one who has departed repose, where souls
of the righteous rest in eternal remembrance.
O most pure one, amid the righteous, present him
as heir of divine blessings.

Glory to the Father and to the Son and to the Holy Spirit.

"As you see me set before you
 Mute and without breath
 Weep for me—O my brethren,
 O my family, and all who know me.
 I spoke with you but yesterday,
 And suddenly the fearful hour
 Did come upon me.
 Come all those who love me
 Give me your last kiss,
 For never again shall I journey

Or talk with you
Until the end of time.
I go to a Judge Who is impartial,
Where servant and master stand
Side by side. King and soldier,
Rich and poor, where all are held
In equal esteem. For each will be
Glorified by his own deeds
Or will be put to shame.
So, I plead and implore you all
To pray ceaselessly to Christ our God,
That I may not be left in searing
Chagrin because of my sins,
But that He may appoint me
To a place bearing the light of life."

Now and ever and unto ages of ages. Amen.

Through the prayers of her who bore You, O Christ,
And of Your forerunner and apostles, Your prophets,
hierarchs, the pious and the righteous, and of all Your saints,
Give rest to Your servant who has fallen asleep.

Glory to You, O God. Amen. Amen. Amen.

Translated from the Greek by Scott Cairns

THE DREAM OF THE ROOD is an Old English poem that was probably written in the 7th or 8th century.

Listen! When lapped in rest   lay all who speak,
to me in a vision   in the middle of the night
came the choicest of dreams,   as I wish to recount.
Seemed to me that I saw   one most splendid tree
arise into the air   enwound with light,
beam-brightest, a beacon   all beglazed with gold
showered upon it,   with shimmering jewels
(like the five that shone   up on the shoulder-span)
at its foot, on the earth—   no felon's gallows, that,
but made lovely by the fore-shaping   of the Lord of the hosts
who beheld it there,   the hallowed, the angels,
with men the world over,   and all this marvelous creation.

Wondrous was the victory-wood,   and I, wounded with sins,
gashed, stained by guilt.   I saw the tree of glory
robed in reverence   and rays of joy,
garbed all in gold,   with goodly gems
like the wrapping of lacework   to honor the Ruler's tree.
Yet through that gold I glimpsed   the grievous strife
endured by doomed men of old,   as drops of blood sweat
from the heart's strong side.   With sorrow was I stirred,
shook before that sight so fair,   for I saw that shimmering sign
change color and cloth,   now clotted with the wet,
drenched in the running blood;   now decked out in treasure.

Still I lay there.   a long while, beheld
raw-hearted with cares,   the Healer's tree,
sign of the Savior,   till I heard it speak out;
the best of all wood   with these words began:

"It was years ago—   as I yet call to mind—
when I was hewn down   at the holt's end,
stripped up from my roots.   Strong men seized me, men of hate,
carved me into a spectacle, commanded me   to carry their criminals;
enemies enough bore me on their shoulders   till on the bald mount
   they set me,
planted me fast.   Then I saw, full of heart,
mankind's Master make haste   that he might climb upon me.
Then I dared not,   against the dread Chieftain's words,
bend or break,   when I beheld the ground trembling;
could have felled   all those foes beneath,
struck them down,   but I stood fast.

"Then the young Hero ungirt himself—   that was God almighty—
strong, stiff-willed,   and strode to the gallows,
climbed stout-hearted in the sight of many;   intended to set men free.
I trembled when the bold Warrior embraced me,   yet I dared not bend
   to the earth,
fall to the ground for fear;   to stand fast was my duty.
A rood was I reared up,   bore the rich King,
the Guardian of heaven;   I dared not give in.
They drove me through with dark spikes,   deep wounds could be seen
   upon me,
open envy-thrusts,   yet not a one of them dared I harm.
Both of us did they mock.   I was bedrenched with blood
spilled from the side of the Man   as he sent up his spirit.
On that mount I endured   many agonies,
words of wrath,   saw racked in pain
the God of hosts.   Then a gloom fell
and clouds shrouded   the corpse of the all-Wielder,
its shimmering sheen;   a shadow went forth,
wan, under the clouds.   Then all God's creatures wept,
lamented the King's fall: Christ was on the cross.

"Nevertheless from afar   to the noble Earl
eager men hastened;   I beheld it all.
Stirred I was with deep sorrows,   still I bowed to the men's hands,
humbly, brave of heart.   Then from the heavy torments they took him,

67

bore away almighty God.   The battle-grooms abandoned me there,
standing spike-pierced   and spattered with blood.
They led him, limb-weary, away;   beheld the Lord of heaven,
stood by his body, at his head,   as, tired after the great strife,
he lay to rest awhile.   Then they wrought for him an earth-house,
fighting men, in sight of the killer,   carved it of bright stone,
laid in it the Lord of victories.   A lay of sorrow they sang him,
grieving, as evening fell.   From the glorious Prince they now parted,
wearily; there he rested, few   of his band of warriors near.
But we three crosses wept   for a good while, standing
where we had been set,   as the song went up
from the bravers of battle.   The body cooled,
fair fortress of life.   Then felled were we all
to the hard earth—   a horrible fate!
They dug us a deep pit;   but the dear thanes of the Lord,
his friends sought me out   and found where I was buried,
and girt me thereafter   in gold and silver.

"Now, my good man,   you may hear tell
that I have borne   bale-dwellers' deeds,
terrible troubles.   Now the time has come
that I am honored   from east to west
by men the world over   and by all this marvelous creation,
beseeching this beacon in prayer.   On me the brave Son of God
suffered awhile;   therefore wondrous I now
tower high beneath the heavens,   and have the might to heal
any man of them all   who meets me with awe.
I had been hewn once.   as the hardest of torments,
most loathsome to men,   till I lay clear
the right road of life   for the race of mankind.
Listen! The Ancient of glory   exalted me then
over all the wood of the forest,   the Watcher of heaven's kingdom,
as he did once for his mother,   Mary herself,
almighty God,   for the good of all men,
granting her worth   above all womankind.

"Now, my dear man,   this duty I give you,
that you say to men   what you have seen tonight,

unwind in words   that it is the wood of glory,
the same that almighty God   suffered upon
for mankind's.   many sins
and for Adam's   ancient deed.
Death's fruit Adam tasted;   but after him the Lord
rose in his great might   for man's salvation.
Then he ascended to the heavens.   Here he will come again
to this middle-garden   to seek mankind
on the day of doom,   the dread Lord himself,
amidst his angels,   almighty God,
intending then to judge,   for the power of judgment is his,
what every man   will have earned for himself,
living here   in this lean short life.
There may no man   remain unafraid
of whatever word   the all-Wielder shall utter;
he shall seek among the many   where that man should be
who would willingly die   for the name of his Lord,
taste the same bitter death   he once endured on the tree.
But no man then   shall need to fear
who bears in his breast   the best of signs,
for he shall come, through the cross,   to that kingdom he seeks,
every soul   from the earth-way,
who longs to dwell   with the Lord almighty."

Light-spirited then I turned   to the tree in prayer,
full of heart, bold,   where with few fellows
I lay alone.   Leaned my mind now,
made eager for the forth-way,   for it had felt many
a longing-hour.   It is now my life's joy
that I may try to seek   the tree of triumph
once more often   than all other men,
to honor it well;   my will to do that
burns warm in my heart,   and my hope, my salvation is
turned right to the Cross.
      For I cannot boast
of rich friends on the earth,   but forth have they gone,
fled the world's joys,   wished to find the King of glory,
are home now in heaven   with the High Father,

dwelling in glory,   and every day I look
forth for that time   when the tree of the Lord,
which here on earth   I have once beheld,
shall lead me away   from this lean short life
and bring me where   the bliss is great,
the joys of heaven,   where joined for the feast
sit the folk of the Lord,   and bliss is forever,
and seat me then   where ever thereafter
I may dwell in glory,   delighting in joys
with the holy saints.   Let him who on earth
suffered once   for the sins of men
on the felon's wood   be a friend to me,
for he loosed our bonds,   gave us life again,
a heavenly home.   Hope was made new,
with blessings and bliss   for those who had burned in the fire;
the Son on that journey   stood victory-fast,
mighty, triumphant,   when amain with a host
of spirits he came   to the kingdom of God,
the one-Wielder almighty,   for his angels' joy
and the happiness of all the hallows   who in heaven already
had been dwelling in glory,   when God almighty,
their Lord, returned   to his land, his home.

Translated from the Old English by Anthony M. Esolen

ALCUIN (c. 735–804) was an English scholar, clergyman, poet, and teacher. He was born in Northumbria and educated at York Cathedral. He then joined the court of Charlemagne at Aachen as its leading scholar. He died at Marmoutier Abbey in Tours.

CONCERNING A NIGHTINGALE

Jealousy, that's what it was. It was thin-fingered envy that nabbed you,
  stealing away my delight, Nightingale, out of the broom!
Sour as my soul had become, you could fill it with honeying sweetness,
  lilting it into my ears, lifting it into my heart.
Come, all you creatures with wings! Let them come from the corners of
  heaven
    adding their grief to my own, singing the song of the muse.
Not much to look at for color, but sound that could carry my heart off:
  sound with the breadth of the air poured from your throat's little strait,
sweetness in dollops and pours and melismas, repeating, renewing,
  always a song in your mouth to him who is maker of all.
Everywhere night and its terrible blackness, yet still you were singing,
  voice that should still us to prayer, ornament hung on the dark.
Why should we wonder at all at the angels eternally chanting
  praise to the Lord of the storm? You could sing endlessly too.

Translated from the Latin by Maryann Corbett

How my thoughts betray me!
    How they flit and stray!
Well they may appal me
    On great judgment day.

Through the psalms they wander
    Roads that are not right;
Mitching, shouting, squabbling
    In God's very sight.

Through august assemblies
    Groups of gamesome girls,
Then through woods, through cities,
    Like the wind in whirls.

Now down lordly highways
    Boisterously they stride,
Then through desert pathways
    Secretly they glide.

In their whims unferried
    Overseas they fly.
Or in one swift motion
    Spin from earth to sky.

Lost to recollection
    Near and far they roam;
From some monstrous errand
    Slyly they slink home.

Where are ropes to bind them?
    Who has fetters fit?
They who lack all patience
    Cannot stand or sit.

No sharp sword affrights them,
    Nor any threatening whip;
Like an eel's tail, greasy,
    From my grasp they slip.

Lock nor frowning dungeon,
    Nor sentinelled frontier,
Townwall, sea nor fortress
    Halts their mad career.

Christ the chaste, the cherished,
    Searcher of the soul,
Grant the seven-fold spirit
    Keep them in control.

Rule my thoughts and feelings,
    You who brook no ill;
Make me yours forever,
    Bend me to your will.

Grant me, Christ, to reach you,
    With you let me be
Who are not frail nor fickle
    Nor feeble-willed like me.

Translated from the Irish by Frank O'Connor

St. Gregory of Narek (c. 950–1003/1011) was an Armenian theologian, priest, monk and poet. He was born in a village on the southern shores of Lake Van, in modern-day Turkey, into a family closely related to the Artsruni royal house. He lived most of his life at the monastery of Narek, where he taught theology.

The Book of Lamentations

Prayer 12

Speaking with God from the Depths of the Heart

A
Although I have let myself fall
into seemingly eternal despair,
beating myself with the rod of doubt,
let me now dare with the slightest hope
to call upon the Holy Trinity to help me, a sinner.
For upon blessing and acknowledging
the life-giving God of all, and calling out to him
as to a family member,
it becomes possible for the benefactor
who grants all grace, to grant life
to me, a mortal, as the Prophet foretold,
"Whoever calls out the name of the Lord shall live."

B
Not only do I call, but I believe in the Lord's greatness.
I pray not only for his rewards but also for himself,
the essence of life, guarantor of giving and
taking of breath
without whom there is no movement, no progress,
to whom I am tied not so much by the knot of hope
as by the bonds of love.

I long not so much for the gifts
as for the giver.
I yearn not so much for the glory
as the glorified.
I burn not so much with the desire for life
as in memory of the giver of life.
I sigh not so much with the rapture of splendor
as with the heartfelt fervor for its maker.
I seek not so much for rest
as for the face of our comforter.
I pine not so much for the bridal feast
as for the distress of the groom,
through whose strength I wait with certain
expectation believing with unwavering hope
that in spite of the weight of my transgressions
I shall be saved by the Lord's mighty hand and
that I will not only receive remission of sins
but that I will see the Lord himself
in his mercy and compassion
and receive the legacy of heaven
although I richly deserve to be disowned.

C
Now for my many humiliations
my head bowed in shame
my lips locked with embarrassment
my tongue not daring to move
I resort again to intoning supplications,
mournful sobs and cries, offered on high.

Accept with sweetness almighty Lord my bitter prayers.
Look with pity upon my mournful face.
Dispel, all-bestowing God, my shameful sadness.
Lift, merciful God, my unbearable burden.
Cast off, potent God, my mortal habits.
Spoil, triumphant God, my wayward pleasures.
Dissipate, exalted God, my wanton fog.
Block, life-giving God, my destructive ways.

Undo, secret-seeing God, my evil entrapments.
Fend off, inscrutable God, my assailants.
Inscribe your name on the skylight of my abode.
Cover the roof of my temple with your hand.
Mark the threshold of my cell with your blood.
Imprint the outside of my door with your sign.
Protect the mat where I rest with your right hand.
Keep my cot pure from all seductions.
Preserve my suffering soul by your will.
Steady the breath of life you have given my flesh.
Surround me with your heavenly host.
Post them on watch against the battalion of demons.

D
Grant blissful rest
like the slumber of death
in the depth of this night
through the intercession of the Holy Mother of
God and the elect.
Firmly close the windows of sight,
sentient faculty of the mind,
with impregnable fortifications
against the waves of anxiety,
the cares of daily life,
nightmares, frenzy, hallucinations,
and protected by the memory of your hope
to wake again from the heaviness of sleep
into alert wakefulness and
soul-renewing cheerfulness
to stand before you
raising my prayerful voice
in harmony with the heavenly choirs of praise
with the fragrance of faith,
to you in heaven, all blessed king,
whose glory is beyond telling.
For you are glorified by all creation
forever and ever.
Amen.

Prayer 46

Speaking with God from the Depths of the Heart

A
Now I am lost, forever punishable,
always immoral,
condemning myself to death,
shepherd of a flock of fetid sin, a flock of wild boars,
a despicable mercenary,
a shepherd watching a flock of desert goats.
The image of the shepherds' tent in the Song of Songs
aptly applies to me,
for I do not know or understand,
by whom, in whose image or why I was created.

B
Behold, you were formed like an angel,
on two feet that take and bring you,
as if in flight on two wings lifting you upward,
to gaze down on my fatherland.
O fool, why did you choose to be earthbound,
always preoccupied with the worldliness of
the here and now,
carrying on like wild asses in the desert?
On the lamp stand of your body, encircling your head,
a chandelier with many arms was placed,
so that by its light you might not stray and might
see God and know what is everlasting.
You were doubly endowed in the womb of reason,
so that you might speak with an unfettered tongue
of the victory of the good things given you.
And you were endowed with artful hands and
nimble fingers
to carry out the practical affairs of daily life
like the all-giving right hand of God,
that you might be called God.
You are assembled of 360 parts and five senses,
the number of the days of the year,

and no aspect of your physical being remains invisible
to your sight or unstudied by your mind.
For some parts are thick and strong,
some are small and others necessary,
some are sturdy but sensitive,
some are sublime, important and noble,
some are necessary but humble,
and the explanation of the image of these things is engraved on you
as on an uneraseable monument, wretched soul of mine,
so that like the elements of time
and the continuous train of days around the year
by some inner law these parts function
in unerring and inalterable order.

C
And now another spiritual image,
tied to the bonds of love uniting the church,
is also reflected within you.
Like the yoke that mediates between the great
and the lowly,
the assembled body
established in the name of Christ is sometimes impaired,
as with the cutting off or loss of an unruly organ,
infecting the body.
Something is lost in your mortal structure,
feeling abode of mankind,
and the usual shape of the person undergoes
some disfigurement.
And now when the uniquely miraculous structure
in the living image of God,
is completely condemned, my enslaved soul,
that original likeness is stolen from you as
by breaking the law in the Garden of Eden.
But by the light of the baptismal font
the breath of the Holy Spirit is received and
the image is restored to God's likeness.

D

And now, why did you give up heavenly glory
like the original man Adam did in the earthly
Garden of Eden?
Why did you yourself close heaven and lock
the door to ascent?
Why did you mix the clean water with
impurities of bitter tears?
Why did you soil newly washed clothes with dirty work?
Why did you put off the clothes given you
and put on the cloak of sin?
Why did you infect the purity of your feet
by taking the path of the fallen?
Why did you repeat the violation of just vows of
the Old Testament?
Why did you refuse the fruit of grace, as Adam did
the tree of life?
Why did you willfully lose the unshadowed hope
of eternity?
Why did you cover your face with brazen shame?
Why did you arm your enemies against you,
repository of stupidity?
Why did you venture into the snares of death,
abandoning the way of faith?
Why did you get caught on the fishhook of deception,
you who share the body of the life giver?
But again, relying upon him, call to him,
the redeemer of those seeking refuge, renewer,
savior, life maker and life giver,
merciful, caring, lover of humanity,
ungrudging, generously compassionate,
blessed forever.
Amen.

Translated from the Armenian by Thomas J. Samuelian

Mael Ísu Ua Brolcháin (d. 1086) was an Irish cleric, scholar and poet. He came from a prominent family in Donegal and was educated at the monastery of Both Chonais. He lived most of his life as a teacher in the cathedral city of Armagh, but later moved to Lismore in the far south, where he died.

A Priest Rediscovers His Psalm-Book

How good to hear your voice again,
    Old love, no longer young, but true,
As when in Ulster I grew up
    And we were bedmates, I and you.

When first they put us twain to bed,
    My love who speaks the tongue of Heaven
I was a boy with no bad thoughts,
    A modest youth, and barely seven.

We wandered Ireland over then,
    Our souls and bodies free of blame,
My foolish face aglow with love,
    An idiot without fear of blame.

Yours was the counsel that I sought
    Wherever we went wandering:
Better I found your subtle thought
    Than idle converse with some king.

You slept with four men after that,
    Yet never sinned in leaving me,
And now a virgin you return—
    I say but what all men can see.

For safe within my arms again,
　　Weary of wandering many ways,
The face I love is shadowed now
　　Though lust attends not its last days.

Faultless my old love seeks me out;
　　I welcome her with joyous heart—
My dear, you would not have me lost,
　　With you I'll learn that holy art.

Since all the world your praises sings,
　　And all acclaim your wanderings past
I have but to heed your counsel sweet
　　To find myself with God at last.

You are a token and a sign
　　To men of what all men must heed;
Each day your lovers learn anew
　　God's praise is all the skill they need.

So may He grant me by your grace
　　A quiet end, an easy mind,
And light my pathway with His face
　　When the dead flesh is left behind.

Translated from the Irish by Frank O'Connor

St. Nerses IV the Gracious (1102–1173) was an Armenian bishop, theologian and poet. He was born into a noble family in the capital city of Hromkla (present-day Rumkale in eastern Turkey) and was ordained as a priest at age 17. He was head of the Armenian church from 1166 to 1173.

Jesus the Son

From Book One

Creator of the hearts, O Lord, thou alone
Who dost see all deeds and thoughts,
Didst put to the test thy beloved,
To sacrifice his son unto thee;
Thou didst bid him go to a high mountain
At Golgotha, in accordance with thy word,
Taking the wood for the burnt offering
Of his only son, so pure in mind.
There he laid him upon the alter,
Like unto thee, O Lord, upon the cross,
He stretched forth his hand, took the knife,
And brought it high unto his throat,
When a voice called out from above:
Lay not thine hand upon that lad,
But behold upon thy right
A ram caught in a thicket,
Which, in the stead of thy servant Isaac,
He who is endowed with reason,
Offer thou as a sacrificial offering
The beast created with no reasoning power.
Do not test me, O Lord, like unto him:
I who am not yet tested by favors,
I who am tested by evil instead,
And am impatient when tested.
For I am neither silver nor gold,

When tested by fire in a crucible;
But am the tin alloyed with lead,
That both perish when thus assayed.
And I am not a rock beside the sea
That stands unshaken against the waves;
Nor am I the deep roots of trees
That are not torn out by gales.
But I am like unto a wrecked ship,
Tossed about upon the high seas;
Or the withered grass lashed away
By the strong autumnal winds.

Thou who dost not tempt the earth-born
For though thou art not tempted with evil,
We ourselves are tempted, as it is told.
But hasten thou to deliver me
From the temptations of the tyrant,
Like unto the father of the faithful
From the snares of the tempter.
That I may sacrifice joyfully
My body, my soul, and my mind,
As a living victim unto thee,
Immortal One, pleasing, holy, and divine.

The younger son, born
Of Isaac and Rebecca,
Thou didst name thy beloved
And didst change Jacob unto Israel.
Thou didst show the future unto him
With a ladder set up from earth to heaven,
Above which the Lord stood watching
And the angels ascended and descended on it.
He poured oil upon the top of the stone
And called it the house of God,
In the likeness of the great mystery
That holy men have revealed;
And he wrestled throughout the night,
As it is written in the Holy Scriptures,

Resisting until the break of day,
Though he was overcome in body.
Now, I am the junior in good deeds,
But fully-grown in evil ones:
Like unto Esau, who was born the first,
But in soul, he was the last.
I sold such priceless treasures
That I may gratify my belly.
And voluntarily erased myself
From the first-born inscribed in heaven.
I implore thee, O Lord on high,
O thou Prince of the celestial choir,
May the gates of heaven open unto me also,
As they did at that time unto Israel.
O raise up my fallen soul
Through the ladder formed of light,
Brought as an example of how men
May return from earth unto heaven.
With the fragrant oil to anoint the soul,
That I lost when deceived by the evil one,
Anoint my head once more
With thy protective right hand.
I cannot resist against thy strength
In wrestling like unto Jacob:
For even with my weak self
I fell into the hands of the evil one.
Extend thy celestial right hand:
Come unto mine aid in my combat
And demolish mine enemy,
That he may never rise to his feet again.

Sons were born unto the patriarch
To become the twelve tribal chiefs;
And eleven of them did betray Joseph,
Delivering him unto the Ismaelites,
They sold their own brother
For thirty pieces of silver,
Like unto thy very disciple,

That was stealthy, treacherous Judas.
Thou wast sold, O Lord, like unto him
As a slave in the house of Potiphar,
And didst save from the Egyptian woman
The pure soul of the chaste youth;
Thou didst enter the Pharaoh's prison,
Didst produce dreams in the night,
And didst have Joseph released thereby
And made ruler over the land.
Likewise, my mother's sons did conspire
Stealthily against me with treachery:
Through my multiple vices on sin,
They sold me at a very low price.
Although I complied with the evil one's will
By not opposing against him,
He did imprison me, nevertheless,
In a dark dungeon with no escape.
But thou, who in spite of everything.
Didst rescue Joseph from the hopeless place,
Deliver me also, O Lord, like unto him,
From the various vices of evil:
Do not deliver me unto the lewd harlot,
Unto the lecherous Egyptian woman;
That which creepeth like unto a serpent
And roareth like unto a lion.
But elevate me above them
And make me ruler of the land of Egypt,
That I may vanquish the evil prince,
That is the invisible tyrant.
And when they come to die of starvation,
Turn me into the house of the bread of life;
That I may distribute it and satiate
Those that yearn for the immortal word.

Translated from the Armenian by Mischa Kudian

St. Francis of Assisi (1181/1182 –1226) was an Italian friar, mystic and preacher who devoted himself to a life of poverty and founded the Franciscan Order.

His Blessings and His Praise (Canticle of the Sun)

To You belong all praises, all honor
and every blessing, though no man
is worthy to so much as speak
Your name. We praise You in the face
of every creature—most especially
Brother Sun who spans our days,
by whom You give us light. His splendor,
radiant and beautiful, bears Your likeness.
You are praised through Sister Moon
and all attendant stars. In their beauty
and clear light we see Your hand.
You are praised through Brother Wind
and through the skies, the cloud-filled
and the calm, and You are praised
through every shade of weather
by which You feed your creatures.
You are praised through Sister Water,
who is willing, modest, precious, and chaste.
You are praised through Brother Fire
by whom You trouble the night; for he
is beautiful, playful, robust, and strong.
You are praised through our Sister Mother Earth,
who feeds and nurtures us, who offers
luscious fruits bearing colored flowers and herbs.
You are praised through those who show mercy
for the love of You, who suffer infirmity
and manifold difficulties with unabated love.
Blessed are all who endure all this in peace,

for You will mark their endurance with a crown.
You are praised through our Sister Bodily Death,
whom no one living can escape. Grief to those
who meet her unrelieved of mortal sin.
Blessed are those whom death will discover
in the midst of Your most holy will, for no
second death shall ever harm them.
All people, praise and bless my Lord, and give
Him thanks, serve Him with deep humility.

Translated from the Italian by Scott Cairns

ARNULF OF LEUVEN (c. 1200–1250) was the abbot of the Cistercian abbey in Villers-la-Ville in present-day Belgium. After serving as abbot for ten years, he abdicated, hoping to devote himself to study and asceticism, but he died soon after. The following poem was long attributed to BERNARD OF CLAIRVAUX (1090–1153), but is more likely by Arnulf.

O SACRED HEAD, NOW WOUNDED

O sacred Head, now wounded, with grief and shame weighed down,
Now scornfully surrounded, with thorns Thine only crown;
O sacred Head, what glory, what bliss till now was Thine!
Yet, though despised and gory, I joy to call Thee mine.

What Thou, my Lord, hast suffered, was all for sinners' gain;
Mine, mine was the transgression, but Thine the deadly pain.
Lo, here I fall, my Saviour! 'Tis I deserve Thy place;
Look on me with Thy favour, vouchsafe to me Thy grace.

Men mock and taunt and jeer Thee, Thou noble countenance,
Though mighty worlds shall fear Thee and flee before Thy glance.
How art thou pale with anguish, with sore abuse and scorn!
How doth Thy visage languish that once was bright as morn!

Now from Thy cheeks has vanished their colour once so fair;
From Thy red lips is banished the splendour that was there.
Grim death, with cruel rigour, hath robbed Thee of Thy life;
Thus Thou hast lost Thy vigour, Thy strength in this sad strife.

My burden in Thy Passion, Lord, Thou hast borne for me,
For it was my transgression which brought this woe on Thee.
I cast me down before Thee, wrath were my rightful lot;
Have mercy, I implore Thee; Redeemer, spurn me not!

What language shall I borrow to thank Thee, dearest friend,
For this Thy dying sorrow, Thy pity without end?
O make me Thine forever, and should I fainting be,
Lord, let me never, never outlive my love to Thee.

My Shepherd, now receive me; my Guardian, own me Thine.
Great blessings Thou didst give me, O source of gifts divine.
Thy lips have often fed me with words of truth and love;
Thy Spirit oft hath led me to heavenly joys above.

Here I will stand beside Thee, from Thee I will not part;
O Saviour, do not chide me! When breaks Thy loving heart,
When soul and body languish in death's cold, cruel grasp,
Then, in Thy deepest anguish, Thee in mine arms I'll clasp.

The joy can never be spoken, above all joys beside,
When in Thy body broken I thus with safety hide.
O Lord of Life, desiring Thy glory now to see,
Beside Thy cross expiring, I'd breathe my soul to Thee.

My Saviour, be Thou near me when death is at my door;
Then let Thy presence cheer me, forsake me nevermore!
When soul and body languish, oh, leave me not alone,
But take away mine anguish by virtue of Thine own!

Be Thou my consolation, my shield when I must die;
Remind me of Thy passion when my last hour draws nigh.
Mine eyes shall then behold Thee, upon Thy cross shall dwell,
My heart by faith enfolds Thee. Who dieth thus dies well.

Translated from Paul Gerhardt's German translation
of the original Latin by J.W. Alexander

St. Thomas Aquinas (1225–1274) was an Italian Dominican friar, theologian and philosopher. He was born near Aquino in central Italy and educated at the Universities of Naples and Paris. He taught theology in Paris, Naples, Orvieto, and Rome. Along with St. Augustine, he is widely considered the greatest of Christian philosophers.

Adoro Te Devote

Godhead here in hiding, whom I do adore,
Masked by these bare shadows, shape and nothing more,
See, Lord, at thy service low lies here a heart
Lost, all lost in wonder at the God thou art.

Seeing, touching, tasting are in thee deceived:
How says trusty hearing? that shall be believed;
What God's Son has told me, take for truth I do;
Truth himself speaks truly or there's nothing true.

On the cross thy godhead made no sign to men,
Here thy very manhood steals from human ken:
Both are my confession, both are my belief,
And I pray the prayer of the dying thief.

I am not like Thomas, wounds I cannot see,
But can plainly call thee Lord and God as he;
Let me to a deeper faith daily nearer move,
Daily make me harder hope and dearer love.

O thou our reminder of Christ crucified,
Living Bread, the life of us for whom he died,
Lend this life to me then: feed and feast my mind,
There be thou the sweetness man was meant to find.

Bring the tender tale true of the Pelican;
Bathe me, Jesu Lord, in what thy bosom ran—
Blood whereof a single drop has power to win
All the world forgiveness of its world of sin.

Jesu, whom I look at shrouded here below,
I beseech thee send me what I thirst for so,
Some day to gaze on thee face to face in light
And be blest for ever with thy glory's sight. Amen.

Translated from the Latin by Gerard Manley Hopkins

DANTE ALIGHIERI (c. 1265–1321) was an Italian poet, philosopher and politician. He was born in Florence, but was exiled from the city in 1302 and never returned. He spent the rest of his life moving from city to city in Italy and died in Ravenna.

THE DIVINE COMEDY

Purgatory

From Canto 3

[Dante and Virgil are about to meet the souls in Ante-Purgatory.]

And in a sudden panic I wheeled round—
   I thought I'd been abandoned, for I saw
   only one shadow darkening the ground.
And then my strength, my comfort, said to me,
   "Even now, such little faith? Don't you believe
   that I am with you, and will guide your way?
The evening falls already by that tomb
   where lies the body that once cast my shadow,
   for Naples took it from Brundisium.
Thus if no shadow follows where I go,
   it's no more wondrous than that heavenly light
   shines unencumbered by the spheres below.
To suffer the tormenting fire and ice
   the Power assigns us bodies that are like,
   but never wills to show us how He does,
For, trusting to man's reason, mad is he
   who hopes to plumb the endless ways of those
   three Persons in substantial Unity.
Be satisfied with 'So it is,' O Man,
   for if you could have known the whole design,
   Mary would not have had to bear a son;

And you've seen men desire in vain before,
    whose intellects might well have calmed the yearning
    that now is made their sorrow evermore:
I speak of Aristotle and of Plato
    and many others," and he bowed his head,
    troubled, and did not say another word.

Paradise

Canto 33

[Saint Bernard entreats the intercession of the Virgin Mary that Dante may behold the beatific vision. The great journey and the poem end with the vision of the three great mysteries: the Creation, the Trinity, and the Incarnation of Christ.]

"Virgin Mother, daughter of your Son,
    humbler and loftier past creation's measure,
    the fulcrum of the everlasting plan,
You are she who ennobled human nature
    so highly, that its Maker did not scorn
    to make Himself the Creature of His creature.
In your womb was the flame of love reborn,
    in the eternal peace of whose warm ray
    this flower has sprung and is so richly grown.
For us you are the torch of the noonday
    of charity; below, you are the spring
    of ever-living hope for men that die.
Lady, so great you are, such strength you bring,
    who does not run to you and looks for grace,
    his wish would seek to fly without a wing.
Not only does your kindness come to brace
    our courage when we beg: often your free
    favor arrives before our prayer's race.
In you is mercy, in you is piety,
    in you magnificence, in you the sum
    of excellence in all things that come to be.
This pilgrim who has witnessed, coming from
    the lowest pool of all the universe,
    the lives of soul and soul in every realm,

Now bends his knee to you, to gain such force
　　by grace, that he may lift his eyes the higher
　　unto his final healing and its source.
And I who never burned in such a fire
　　for my own vision, all I can I pray
　　and hope my prayers suffice for his desire,
That by your prayers you melt the mist away
　　that clouds the intellect of mortal men,
　　in order that the highest bliss display
Himself to him. Also I beg you, Queen,
　　who can do what you will, that his affection
　　may remain pure after what he has seen.
Let human passions yield to your protection.
　　See Beatrice, see how many of the blest
　　now fold their hands to second my intention!"
The eyes beloved of God and honored best,
　　fixed on the man who prayed, showed her delight
　　in prayers that rise from a devoted breast,
And then they turned to the eternal Light,
　　wherein, we trust, no creature else can send
　　created vision with such perfect sight.
And I who now was drawing near the end
　　of all desires, as it behooved me, to
　　the summit let my leaping flames ascend;
Bernard smiled, motioned me to turn my view
　　upward—but I had turned it on my own,
　　was doing what he wanted me to do,
For as my sight grew pure and whole, alone
　　it plumbed more and more deeply into the ray
　　of Truth, the utmost Light. From this point on
Whatever human language can convey
　　must yield to vision, passing the extreme—
　　to such great prowess memory must give way.
As one who sees a vision in a dream,
　　after the dream the passion so impressed
　　lingers, though nothing else comes back to him,
So am I, for the sight is all but lost,
　　and yet, born from that vision, to this day,
　　droplets of sweet distill into my breast.

94

So in the sun the snow dissolves away;
    so did they lose the Sibyl's prophecy
    when the wind blew the weightless leaves astray.
Summit of light that lift yourself so high
    above the mind of mortal man, restore
    some slightest shade of your theophany,
And grant then to my tongue sufficient power
    to leave the palest flicker of your glory
    to readers of a later day and hour,
For should something return to memory
    and sound but faintly in my verses here,
    the clearer will they see your victory.
Should I have turned my vision anywhere
    but to the living Ray, I'd have gone blind,
    so piercing was the powers I had to bear;
Thus was I bolder—this I call to mind—
    to bear the might radiance that bloomed,
    till my might and Omnipotence were joined.
O overbrimming grace whence I presumed
    to gaze upon the everlasting Light
    so fully that my vision was consumed!
I saw the scattered elements unite,
    bound all with love into one book of praise,
    in the deep ocean of the infinite;
Substance and accident and all their ways
    as if breathed into one: and, understand,
    my words are a weak glimmer in the haze.
The universal Being of this band
    I think I saw—because when that is said,
    I feel the bliss within my heart expand.
One instant sees more of my memories fade
    than two millennia fade the bravery
    that made the sea god gape at Argo's shade.
And so my mind, suspended utterly,
    held its gaze still immobile and intent,
    and ever kindled was my wish to see.
Before that Light one's will to turn is spent:
    one is so changed, it is impossible
    to shift the glance, for one would not consent,

Because all good—the object of the will—
    is summed in it, for it alone is best:
    beyond, defection; there, whole, perfect, still.
Even for these few memories I've confessed,
    my words are less than what a baby says
    who wets his tongue still at his mama's breast.
Not that I saw more than a single face
    as I was gazing into the living glow,
    for it is ever as it ever was,
But in my vision winning valor so,
    that sole appearance as I changed by seeing
    appeared to change and form itself anew.
Within that brilliant and profoundest Being
    of the deep light three rings appeared to me,
    three colors and one measure in their gleaming:
As rainbow begets rainbow in the sky,
    so were the first two, and the third, a flame
    that from both rainbows breathed forth equally.
Alas how feeble language is, how lame
    beside my thought!—and, for what I was shown,
    to call thought "small" would be too great a claim.
O Light that dwell within Thyself alone,
    who alone know Thyself, are known, and smile
    with Love upon the Knowing and the Known!
That circle which appeared—in my poor style—
    like a reflected radiance in Thee,
    after my eyes had studied it awhile,
Within, and in its own hue, seemed to be
    tinted with the figure of a Man,
    and so I gazed on it absorbedly.
As a geometer struggles all he can
    to measure out the circle by the square,
    but all his cogitation cannot gain
The principle he lacks: so did I stare
    at this strange sight, to make the image fit
    the aureole, and see it enter there:
But mine were not the feathers for that flight,
    Save that the truth I longed for came to me,
    smiting my mind like lightning flashing bright.

Here ceased the powers of my high fantasy.
　　Already were all my will and my desires
　　turned—as a wheel in equal balance—by
The Love that moves the sun and the other stars.

Translated from the Italian by Anthony M. Esolen

Juan Ruiz, Archpriest of Hita (c. 1283–c. 1350) was a Spanish priest and poet. He was born in Alcalá de Henares, near Madrid. He probably studied in Toledo and may have been imprisoned at some point for unspecified crimes.

From *The Book of Good Love*

Death, I compel my heart to charge you still:
you never comfort men. Fat earthworms will
finish off what's left of those you kill.
Like any toxic weed, you make us ill.

You punish the good eater: his head aches;
your dreadful club no sooner meets than breaks
the toughest head, since strength no difference makes
at all, nor any medicine he takes.

Beautiful eyes you send up to the ceiling,
blind them at once to leave their owner reeling;
his story ends with the hoarse breath you're stealing.
You are all foul, disgusting, cruel, unfeeling.

Now sound and smell and touch and taste and sight—
all five senses—you steal, and their delight.
Who can curse you enough, insult you right?
You've earned our hate: where will you spend the night?

Shame you toss out; the beautiful, undo;
grace you strip bare—order and reason too.
You weaken strength, derange the sane and true,
and turn the sweet to bile, bitter as you.

What's wholesome you despise; you tarnish gold,
cancel creation, turn joy joyless and cold,
stain what was clean, smear courtesy with mould.
Death, you hate life, and earth, our home of old.

You please none, but you hail all those well met
who kill each other and most harm abet;
your club destroys all well-made things; you let
nothing that's born to live escape your net.

Enemy of the good, the bad's best friend,
your nature must toward grief and evil tend.
Sorrow goes where your footsteps often wend,
but less so where your journeys seldom end.

Your home forever is the depths of hell.
You're the first evil, and the next as well.
Your hell you fill vacating where we dwell.
Boasting "I govern all!" you strut and swell.

Death, hell was made for you, your rightful place.
Were men earth-bound forever, then our race
would not fear you, your dwelling, or your face,
nor flesh tremble with fear of your embrace.

You fill graveyards with all the towns you strip,
raise boneyards with the empires you let slip;
saints sing the Psalms with fear on every lip.
Except for God, all fear your wicked whip.

Death, you stripped heaven, left its seats all bare.
Those who were clean—now filthy—fell to where
former angels—now devils—scream and glare,
tending your every whim their only care.

You killed the lord who made you, so to test
Jesus Christ, God and man, whom you distressed.
The lord of earth and heaven, at your behest,
was made to fear and perish like the rest.

Hell fears him; you did not. When you drew near,
his body feared the shape he saw appear—
his flesh, that is, which you encountered here—
but his Godhead, unseen, harbored no fear.

He saw and knew you, though you knew him not.
His death was cruel, his torment defied thought:
it doomed you, hell, and those who there must rot.
He died one hour; death—endless—is your lot.

When he destroyed you, then, too late, you learned.
His pain, a thousand times increased, returned
to you, who killed him who our life had earned
upon the cross, on which you saw him spurned.

The saints were captive in the evil hole
you meant to fill with every life you stole;
thanks to Christ's holy death, with life and soul
retrieved, the saints were saved from your control.

Freed from your torments came our sire, Adam,
and Eve our mother, their sons Shem and Ham
and Japhet; patriarchs, good Abraham,
Isaac, Isaiah; he remembered Dan,

Saint John the Baptist, patriarchs galore
whom you had kept in bonds behind hell's door,
Moses—a galley slave!—who was, before,
our leader; saints and prophets, many more.

I cannot say how many, forced to cower
in hell, you had condemned to be your dower.
Christ took the chosen saints home to his bower,
but left the lost and evil in your power.

His own he raised with him to Paradise
to bask in glory great beyond all price;
he who purchased our life with sacrifice
would rescue us from hell, our savior twice.

As for those evil ones who call you sire,
you punish them in the most painful, dire,
infernal torment, burning in hellfire.
But not forever, though you so desire.

May our God shield us from that horrid state
who did not shield himself, nor hesitate
to save us from your grasp, which soon or late,
however long we live, is our shared fate.

So are you left, Death, all your wealth a crumb,
and none to tally of your works the sum.
I commend me to God, whose martyrdom
alone can save me when you surely come.

Translated from the Spanish by Rhina P. Espaillat

Francesco Petrarca (1304–1374), commonly known as Petrarch, was an Italian scholar, poet and Renaissance humanist. He was born in Arezzo in Tuscany, grew up near Avignon in France and was educated at Montpellier and Bologna. He spent most of his life travelling throughout France and Italy as a scholar and diplomat.

CANZONIERE

81

I was so exhausted by the ancient burden
  of sin and the heart's evil inclinations,
  that I feared I'd weaken on the way
  and fall into our original enemy's hands.
Then the truest friend rescued me—
  his supreme sacrifice unspeakably kind.
  He broke my chains, then vanished on high.
  Now my heart seeks his face everywhere.
His sweet voice still echoes in my heart
  "O you who are heavy burdened, here is the way.
  Come unto me, for I have cleared your path!"
What grace, what love, what divine mercy
  blesses me with the wings of a dove
  and lifts me from earth to find rest above?

365

I'm crying over my past life
    which I wasted loving mortal things
    when I could have ascended on spiritual wings
    and freed my heart of earthly desires.
You, who see my wickedness and sins,
    King of heaven, King of the immortal sky,
    heal my crippled soul
    that your grace may be fulfilled,
so, though I lived among war and storms,
    I may die in port as this vain world vanishes,
    knowing you remember your promises.
Now, in the little life that still remains,
    and at my dying, may your hand be near:
    Lord, you know I have no other hope.

Translated from the Italian by Richard Jones

366

Virgin, so lovely, clothed in the sun's light
and crowned with stars, so pleased the highest Sun
that inside you He chose to hide his light:
love urges me to speak of you in verse,
but I cannot begin without your help
and His who loving placed himself in you.
I call upon the one who always answered
whoever called with faith.
Virgin, if toward mercy
for extreme misery of worldly things
you ever turned, then bend now to my prayer,
and help me in my war,
though I am dust and you are queen of Heaven.

Virgin so wise, one of the lovely number
of all the blessèd, prudent virgins—rather,
the first of them and with the brightest light,
O sturdy shield for all who are afflicted

against the blows that Death and Fortune wield
beneath which they're triumphant, more than saved,
O refuge from blind ardor that is raging
in foolish mortals here.
Virgin, those lovely eyes
that saw in sorrow those pitiless wounds
upon the sweet limbs of your cherished son,
turn my dangerous state,
who come imprudent to you for your help.

Virgin so pure and perfect in all ways,
mother and the daughter both of your own child,
who brighten this life and adorn the other;
through you your Son, Son of the highest Father
(O shining, lofty window of the Heavens)
came down to save us in the final days,
and you among all earthly dwelling places
He chose—and only you.
Virgin so blessed and holy,
who change the tears of Eve to happiness,
make me, for you can, worthy of this grace,
O blessèd without end,
already crowned in the supernal realm.

Virgin so holy, full of every grace,
who through your true and high humility
rose up to Heaven where you hear my prayers,
who brought into this world the Fount of pity,
the Sun of justice who brightens the world
which is so full of error dark and thick;
three sweet and cherished names you have collected:
mother, daughter and bride;
Virgin so glorious,
bride of the King who freed us from our bonds
and made the world a free and happy place,
upon whose holy wounds
I pray, quiet my heart, true Beatrix.

Virgin without an equal in the world,
whose beauty made all Heaven fall in love,
whom no one could surpass or even reach,
your holy thoughts, your actions kind and chaste
prepared a consecrated, living temple
of rich virginity for the true God.
Through you my life can know what joy is like,
if through your prayers, O Mary,
Virgin so sweet and pious,
grace will abound where sin abounded once.
And with the knee of my mind bent in prayer
I beg you be my guide,
direct my twisted path to a good end.

Virgin eternal, bright and stable star
above all this tempestuous sea of ours,
the faithful guide of every faithful helmsman,
consider now how frightening is the storm
I'm caught in all alone without a tiller,
and I am close to my last drowning shouts.
But nonetheless in you my soul still trusts,
though it, no doubt, be sinful,
Virgin, but I beg
you not to let your foe have the last laugh.
Remember that it was our sin made God
take on, for our salvation,
the flesh of man in your virginal cloister.

Virgin, how many tears I've shed already,
how many flattering words and prayers in vain
for nothing but my pain and grievous loss!
Since I was born upon the Arno's banks,
then wandering from one place to another,
my life has always been nothing but trouble.
Mortal beauty, actions, and words are what
have burdened all my soul.
Virgin holy, bountiful,
do not delay, this could be my last year;

my days more swift then arrows have sped off
through wretchedness and sin,
and there is only Death awaiting me.

Virgin, that one is dust and holds in grief
my heart, who while alive kept it in tears
and of my thousand sufferings knew not one;
and even had she known them then, what happened
would still have happened—had she wished otherwise,
it would have meant my death and her dishonor.
Now you, Lady of Heaven, you our Goddess,
(if such a term be fitting),
Virgin of superb senses,
you can see all, and what could not be done
by others is no match for your great power:
end now my suffering
and bring honor to you, to me salvation.

Virgin, in whom I place all of my hope
you can and will help me in my great need:
do not abandon me at the last pass,
not for my sake but His who made me man,
let not my own worth but His own high likeness
in me move you to care for one so low.
Medusa and my sin turned me to stone
dripping useless moisture.
Virgin, now with repentant
and holy tears fill up my weary heart;
at least let my last weeping be devout,
without the mud of earth,
as was the first and insane vow of mine.

Virgin so kind, the enemy of pride,
let love of our same origin move you,
have pity of a sorry, humble heart;
for if a bit of mortal, fleeting dust
can make me love with faith so marvelous,
how then will I love you, a noble thing?

If from my state so wretched and so vile
I rise up at your hands,
Virgin, then in your name
I cleanse and give my thoughts and wit and style,
my tongue and heart, my tears and sighs to you.
Show me a better crossing
and please look kindly on my changed desires.

The day draws near, it cannot be far off;
time runs and flies so fast,
Virgin, the one and only one,
and death and conscience now stab at my heart;
commend me to your Son who is the true
man and the truth of God,
that He accept my final breath in peace.

Translated from the Italian by Mark Musa

DAFYDD AP GWILYM (c. 1315/1320–c. 1350/1370) was a Welsh poet. He is thought to have been born in Llanbadarn Fawr, near Aberystwyth in Cardiganshire. He is further thought to have died of plague during the Black Death.

THE SKYLARK

The skylark every day takes flight
up from his house, by earliest light
rising toward heaven: he, the singer
of golden song, the April-bringer.

Master of rhyme, whose work is sweet,
whose labor is a graceful feat,
the grey-winged skylark sings and roves
above the quiet hazel groves.
Yes, you whose mind and more than speech
have taught you well your faith to preach,
praise God as did Sir Kai, with passion,
visit the stars fitfully flashing,
tracing their motions, pouring song
drawn from the well of strength. How strong
you soar the world—a chapel wide,
where you make music as you glide!
Look how you've done your work, how well
such priceless truths of faith you tell—
or rather sing—honoring God,
and how you've garnered your reward!

Let every virtuous being praise
his Maker and His pristine ways,
as He decrees. Praise Him forever,
as thousands do; forget Him never.

Singer of love songs—author too,
in gray-brown garments—where are you?
Your voice is gentle, pure and clear;
your songs, inspired: a joy to hear.
You are—good omen!—hence to be
a cantor to the Deity,
with skill and privileges blessed,
and, if wide-capped, wear a grey crest.
Rise and discover, songful bird,
that unspoiled place, and there be heard!

After you're safely there, one day—
the longest of the year—you may
notice a man who seems aware
of who you are and why you're there.
He'll say that God, the One in Three,
will not consign you to a tree,
but keep you close, to show His face
and share His miracles and grace.

Singer of praise for countless things,
come down, with blessings on your wings,
and be my envoy, brother mine
Go to my lady with a sign,
to greet her and her many graces.
Fair as Gwynedd's moon her face is!
Beg of her a kiss—or two—
and bring those back to me brand new.
Lord of that airy sea beside
her court, where I would gladly bide
with her forever from this day,
let rivals rage as rage they may.

For killing you, the fine is such
that you need fear no creature's touch.
Envious Jaloux might think of trying;
It's he who'd face the fear of dying!
The sky is yours: a comfy perch

where you're as safe as one in church,
far from the arrow and the bow,
where he—Jaloux, seething below—
cursing his rival, passes by,
and never more be moved to try.

Translated from the Welsh by Rhina P. Espaillat with Rowan Williams

HENSA KRESTOS (15th century), assuming that is the name of the poet, was an Ethiopian monk and poet. Nothing else is known about him.

FROM *THE HARP OF GLORY*

In the name of God the Father, who made you the bearer of the jewel of
his heart,
And in the name of God the Son, who veiled himself with your flesh,
And in the name of God the Holy Spirit whose wings came over you in
greeting,
I sing to you my Lady Mary, a sweet song and a graceful poem.
Once more I bring you the fruit of my lips.
O Bride, since you were always devoid of carnal knowledge,
And since you were the shelter of the Father of Lights,
You are rightly named the Dove;
For you brought good news with the wondrous fresh branch.
You are called the Turtle Dove; and the Queen Bee that gives pure honey.
You are called the Ark, to whom the Cherubim offer their shade.
You are the Table carrying the oblation and the holocaust.
You are called the Dish, brimming with milk.
You are called the Chalice of wine, that brings joy to the heart.
You are called the Purification, and the hyssop of sprinkling,
Which sanctifies that which is sordid, and purifies that which is defiled.

O Virgin, the proper celebration of your purity
Is beyond the ability of this stammering tongue.
If I were full of knowledge and abounded in wisdom like Solomon,
Or if the spirit of Elijah was found once more in me,
As it was in Elisha when he cleansed the blemishes of Naaman with his
word,
Or if like Sutael I could drink a river the color of fire,
Or if the branches of my understanding extended and spread to the ends
of the earth,

111

And if all my hairs and all my bones were to be turned into spiritual
  tongues,
Or if the pen of my mind were truly exercised in the art of composition,
Even then I could not possibly reach the limit of your appropriate praises,
For they are greater even than the number of the stars, or the drops of
  falling rain,
And no one can ever count them or estimate them.

O Virgin who brought forth the stems
Bring me safely through precipitous lands, and through the dangerous
  place.
Make me your companion, the fellow traveler at your side.

My Lady Mary—
Bearer of the Sun of Justice
Whence he brought forth his glorious beauty,
And let his rays shine out upon the whole heaven's circuit.
You are the sacred vestment, the vesture of the High Priest
Which he wore in the sanctum when he prayed
For his own sins and those of the people.

You are the Tabernacle of the Most High,
The House of the Wisdom of His Son,
Above which the sound of his voice issued forth and was heard,
And where the Cherubim meet one another with touching wings.
You are the medicinal pool, in which the sick wash themselves,
Those who lie in the portico of faith.
You are the net cast out into the vastness of the sea of this world,
Which the fishers stretch out to capture the fish of souls.
You are the prize of all our race; and give reward even to the animals.
O Virgin, because of you the sorrowing are made merry.
The oppressed are liberated; those who are dead come back to life.
Those who are lost are found again by you,
And those who are far off are brought near.
Those who have fallen are drawn up once more by the rope of your love.
Those who have been scattered, you draw together again.
Those who are oppressed find and discover their peace in you.

O Cloud, the raindrops of your compassion water the desert hills,
And the shrubs in the wilderness are refreshed.
Because of your dew, the trees of the orchard flourish and give fruit.
O Virgin, you are the winepress of the vintage of rejoicing,
And the spring of the water of happiness.
By your assistance deliver me from the distress and the troubles of this
    age,
And grant me to recline at the wedding banquet of your Son
In the company of his faithful who multiplied the gold talent.

My Lady Mary—
Tabernacle of Belseel and Ooliab,
Covered with the cloud and robed in the splendor of fire,
You are the Candlestick facing North, and the Table facing West.
You are the Ark, not made by any human skill, but by the Holy Spirit.
You are the basin, not made by an artisan, but by God himself,
Which with the water of sanctity and purity, made ablution for all the filth
    of sin.

O Granary of Joseph,
You are the Benediction which made Gad greater.
It was you who conferred the consecration on Levi,
And enriched the treasury of the King of Judah.
You are the priestly robe of Aaron that tinkled with bells.
O Ewe-Sheep, Mother of the Spiritual Lamb,
The Archangels praise you, the Heavenly Powers glorify you.
Turn your wise and knowing eyes upon me;
By your ready help and your righteousness, make me wise.
Let me suck at the breast of learning;
And then I shall expand on the praises of your kingdom.
Engrave on the tablets of my heart the life-giving precepts of your Son.
My Queen, be ever quick to help and deliver me.
Encompass me with a defense and guard my life.
Preserve my days that remain, and in your righteousness comfort me.

My Lady Mary—
You are the pleasant Mandrake of the Land of Laban
Which Reuben, the first-born of Israel, found in the time of harvest,

Which the mildew could never blight, and the arid winds could never
  wither.
You are the Myrrh of Tarshish and the frankincense from Sheba,
So sweet the perfume, across the length and breadth of the world,
From East to West, from the North to the South.
You are the chosen Rod, which blossomed with Almonds,
And which gave the people of Israel a prefigurement of you.
You are the Pool of Siloam, and the Cedar of Lebanon.
The branches of your praise shall reach out to the ends of the earth, and to
  the sea.
O Bride, in you the sister of Solomon rejoiced,
She whose breasts were beautiful.
The one whom, after Oholah and Oholibah,
Your Son espoused to himself.

In you the heavens rejoice and tell forth your majesty,
And the earth is glad, and all those who dwell within its fullness;
The Mountains leap like rams and the hills like nursling lambs.
The sea dresses herself out in your honor,
And the rivers thunder out your praises like applause.
In you righteousness and mercy have found one another,
Justice and faith have embraced.
O Virgin, vessel of pure milk,
Quench the flames of my sadness
And allow me to drink from the fountain of your love.
mercifully protect me from the distress of the time of testing.
Since I have made offering to you of the remainder of my life,
Then be its guardian.

My Lady Mary—
More perfumed than honeysuckle, or the fragrance of myrrh;
More delightful than Topaz, more beautiful by far than Chrysolite,
For inviolate you gave birth to God.
Those on earth give you glory; the angels in heaven rejoice in you,
The chorus of Seraphim praise you, the host of Cherubim proclaim you,
For you gave birth to the Spiritual Lamb.
Now grant to my heart a spirit of wisdom and understanding
And put a guard on my lips.

May your protection ever guide me, and your assistance keep me safe.
Deliver me from evil, and set me free from tribulation.
O Mother, hear my voice, and listen to my cry.

My Lady Mary—
Your name runs with milk and honey.
You are ready like the bee to offer good things,
But your disposition is merciful, like the dove.
The Father made you ready as the dwelling place of his Son
Before ever the earth was made, or the vault of the heavens was set out on
    high,
Before the sun had ever risen, or the brightness of Orion could be seen,
Before the rivers ran, before the waters of the Negev were gathered in.
You are the gift of blessing to Shem,
The grace of Jacob's beauty, the column of witness for Joshua,
The portion of Caleb's inheritance.
You are the Ark, placed between two Cherubim.
You showed your wondrous works in the land of the Philistines
When they led you around (what loss to the house of Abinadab!)
When they offered you their votive offerings of pure golden figures.
You are the Golden wall, the Heavenly Sea of Crystal, whose price is
    inestimable.
You are the Golden Pitcher, by which means the water of wisdom was
    drawn from Horeb.
You are the winepress, that gushed out the wine of gladness,
The Chaste wedding, all immaculate, the Bride Inviolate.
O wise Virgin, I knock at the doorway of your halls.
Open to one who seeks, that I may find.
It is your grace I long for, do not withhold it from me.
My heart's desire is to be sheltered by your right hand,
That my foes may never seize me, like the hungry wolf, or the ravenous
    bear.

My Lady Mary—
Consecrated to virginity from your earliest years,
Whose heart gave no entry to the desires of this world,
There is none among men or angels that can compare with you.
You are the thorn bush that bore the flames of fire,

115

Out of which God himself spoke
About how he would deliver the tent of his people Jacob from it.
You are the Cloud of Manna raining down at the time dew descends
All manner of delightful food, flavored according to each one's taste.
You are the Basket of Figs spoken of in the prophecy
Which the Ethiopian Ebed Melek found in recent times
When he awoke after a sleep of sixty-six years.
O Virgin, in you God set the seal on the vision of the prophets,
For in you the gates of Paradise were re-opened, which the Seraphim were
    guarding.
Your works are truly wonderful,
But cannot be easily explained to those who question them.
Blessed is he who in your name offers a shout of acclaim,
Blessed is the one who day by day offers praise to you unceasingly.
Blessed is he who is guarded by the protection of your prayers.
Evil will never harm him, the time of tribulation will never fall upon him.
The crowds are no terror to him; he will have no care for the uprising of
    enemies.
The time of testing does not cast him down,
And the hour of affliction does not distress him.
O Queen, who exude such sweet perfume, far and wide,
Grant to this supplicant who seeks a reward
A double share in the riches of your Son, for they can never be counted.
Under you wings protect me, and spread your shade above me.

Translated from Mark Van den Oudenrijn's Latin translation
of the original Ge'ez by John A. McGuckin

FRANÇOIS VILLON (c. 1441–c. 1463) was a French poet and criminal. He was born in Paris and studied at the university there. After a long history of thievery and violence, he was banished from the city in 1463, after which his fate is unknown.

BALLADE OF PRAYER TO OUR LADY

in the voice of the poet's mother

Lady of Heaven, who holds earthly sway
And reigns as Empress of the hellish deep,
Receive me, one poor Christian, as I pray
That I may be among your chosen sheep—
This notwithstanding that my value's cheap.
Your graces, Holy Dame, I hardly dare
Think can outweigh the load of sins I bear.
Without such graces, no soul hopes to fly
Upward, nor merit Heaven. So I swear:
In this faith I resolve to live and die.

To your son Jesus, say that I am His.
By Him may all my sins be cancelled out,
Grant pardon as He did the Egyptianess
Or poor Theophilus, for whose erring doubt
You gained acquittal, even though the lout
Bartered his soul to Lucifer—alas!—
Save me from coming to that evil pass,
Virgin untouched, who without plaint or sigh
Carried the Host we honor at each Mass:
In this faith I resolve to live and die.

I am a poor old woman, that is all—
Unschooled, unlettered, and devoid of wit.
My parish church has painted on the wall
A scene of Heaven, and the hellish pit.
The first shows harps and lutes. The second, it
Shows damned souls boiling in the flames' embrace.
Grant me the first, High Goddess of all grace,
To whom all sinners must return and cry
Filled up with faith, not feigning or two-faced:
In this faith I resolve to live and die.

L'Envoi

Virgin high-born and worthy, you gave birth
In piety to the King of Heaven and earth.
Lord Jesus, who took on our paltry worth.
Leaving His place, He came down from on high
Offering up His life to death's cruel mirth.
Now I confess Him Lord, in wealth or dearth.
In this faith I resolve to live and die.

Translated from the French by Joseph S. Salemi

BALLADE OF THE HANGED MEN (VILLON'S EPITAPH)

O brother men who after us remain,
Do not look coldly on the scene you view,
For if you pity wretchedness and pain,
God will the more incline to pity you.
You see us hang here, half a dozen who
Indulged the flesh in every liberty
Till it was pecked and rotted, as you see,
And these our bones to dust and ashes fall.
Let no one mock our sorry company,
But pray to God that He forgive us all.

If we have called you brothers, don't disdain
The appellation, though alas it's true
That not all men are equal as to brain,
And that our crimes and blunders were not few.
Commend us, now that we are dead, unto
The Virgin Mary's son, in hopes that He
Will not be sparing of His clemency,
But save our souls, which Satan would enthrall.
We're dead now, brothers; show your charity
And pray to God that He forgive us all.

We have been rinsed and laundered by the rain,
And by the sunlight dried and blackened too.
Magpie and crow have plucked our eyeballs twain
And cropped our eyebrows and the beards we grew.
Nor have we any rest at all, for to
And fro we sway at the wind's fantasy,
Which has no object, yet would have us be
(Pitted like thimbles) at its beck and call.
Do not aspire to our fraternity,
But pray to God that He forgive us all.

Prince Jesus, we implore Your Majesty
To spare us Hell's distress and obloquy;
We want no part of what may there befall.
And, mortal men, let's have no mockery,
But pray to God that He forgive us all.

Translated from the French by Richard Wilbur

Jorge Manrique (c. 1440–1479) was a Spanish soldier and poet. He was a supporter of Isabel I of Castile in her battle over succession to the throne and died in that conflict.

From *Verses on the Death of My Father*

Let no one fondly dream again,
That Hope and all her shadowy train
Will not decay;
Fleeting as were the dreams of old,
Remembered like a tale that's told,
They pass away.

Our lives are rivers, gliding free
To that unfathomed, boundless sea,
The silent grave!
Thither all earthly pomp and boast
Roll, to be swallowed up and lost
In one dark wave.

Thither the mighty torrents stray,
Thither the brook pursues its way,
And tinkling rill.
There all are equal; side by side
The poor man and the son of pride
Lie calm and still.

I will not here invoke the throng
Of orators and sons of song,
The deathless few;
Fiction entices and deceives,
And, sprinkled o'er her fragrant leaves,
Lies poisonous dew.

To One alone my thoughts arise,
The Eternal Truth, the Good and Wise,
To Him I cry,
Who shared on earth our common lot,
But the world comprehended not
His deity.

This world is but the rugged road
Which leads us to the bright abode
Of peace above;
So let us choose that narrow way,
Which leads no traveller's foot astray
From realms of love.

Our cradle is the starting-place,
In life we run the onward race,
And reach the goal;
When, in the mansions of the blest,
Death leaves to its eternal rest
The weary soul.

Did we but use it as we ought,
This world would school each wandering thought
To its high state.
Faith wings the soul beyond the sky,
Up to that better world on high,
For which we wait.

Yes, the glad messenger of love,
To guide us to our home above,
The Saviour came;
Born amid mortal cares and fears,
He suffered in this vale of tears
A death of shame.

Behold of what delusive worth
The bubbles we pursue on earth,
The shapes we chase
Amid a world of treachery!
They vanish ere death shuts the eye,
And leave no trace.

* * *

"Think not the struggle that draws near
Too terrible for man, nor fear
To meet the foe;
Nor let thy noble spirit grieve,
Its life of glorious fame to leave
On earth below.

"A life of honor and of worth
Has no eternity on earth,
'T is but a name;
And yet its glory far exceeds
That base and sensual life, which leads
To want and shame.

"The eternal life, beyond the sky,
Wealth cannot purchase, nor the high
And proud estate;
The soul in dalliance laid, the spirit
Corrupt with sin, shall not inherit
A joy so great.

"But the good monk, in cloistered cell
Shall gain it by his book and bell,
His prayers and tears;
And the brave knight, whose arm endures
Fierce battle, and against the Moors
His standard rears.

"And thou, brave knight, whose hand has poured
The life-blood of the Pagan horde
O'er all the land,
In heaven shalt thou receive, at length,
The guerdon of thine earthly strength
And dauntless hand.

"Cheered onward by this promise sure,
Strong in the faith entire and pure
Thou dost profess,
Depart, thy hope is certainty,
The third, the better life on high
Shalt thou possess."

"O Death, no more, no more delay;
My spirit longs to flee away,
And be at rest;
The will of Heaven my will shall be,
I bow to the divine decree,
To God's behest.

"My soul is ready to depart,
No thought rebels, the obedient heart
Breathes forth no sigh;
The wish on earth to linger still
Were vain, when 't is God's sovereign will
That we shall die.

"O thou, that for our sins didst take
A human form, and humbly make
Thy home on earth;
Thou, that to thy divinity
A human nature didst ally
By mortal birth,

"And in that form didst suffer here
Torment, and agony, and fear,
So patiently;
By thy redeeming grace alone,
And not for merits of my own,
Oh, pardon me!"

As thus the dying warrior prayed,
Without one gathering mist or shade
Upon his mind;
Encircled by his family,
Watched by affection's gentle eye
So soft and kind;

His soul to Him who gave it rose;
God lead it to its long repose,
Its glorious rest!
And, though the warrior's sun has set,
Its light shall linger round us yet,
Bright, radiant, blest.

Translated from the Spanish by Henry Wadsworth Longfellow

Marko Marulić (1450–1524) was a Croatian poet, lawyer and Renaissance humanist. He was born in Split in Dalmatia into a noble family. After studying law in Italy, he worked as a lawyer and judge in Split. Among his many writings in Latin, Croatian and Italian, are two long poems, *Judith* and *Susanna*, based on stories from the Apocrypha.

From *Judith*

Now it is time to go back to where my story led
before we turned aside to give advice instead.
Holofernes staggered: he'd managed—what a hog!—
to eat enough for two, and then to sleeping like a log.
Bagoas, closing up, called all the others out,
who barely found their way by teetering about,
so soused were they from every brimming jug and cup
they toasted with, while roaring songs they had made up.
And every toast tossed back after a single taste,
then emptied in a hurry and instantly replaced.
Their legs kept giving way under them, tangled so
they tripped over each other, staggered to and fro,
dizzy with fumes, their faces red as flames from hell,
their beards gleaming with grease where shiny droplets fell.
Their fat bellies poked out over their pants like pots;
they couldn't say a word—their tongues were tied in knots—
with heads empty of reason and eyes empty as glass,
laughing over nothing, each seemed a shameless ass.
One fell and crashed into a board; one stood up to piss;
others fought and made a racket over that or this.
Some, when trying to stand up, would try to grab another:
then both would slide down on their backs, brother to brother.
Some made as if to vomit, and some succeeded, too.
They lay on the ground in it, where others stumbled through.
Some had the great good luck to be carried to bed,
with as much common sense as donkeys three days dead.

Those who have enough brains to stay away from greed
  should think about these people, and ponder if indeed
  it's true that honor's died and sin taken its place,
  so even former war heroes may sink into disgrace.
Just look at Holofernes, and notice how he's lost
  his strength through lustful deeds, and calculate the cost!
  His bed was in a chamber that was clean and bright:
  the curtains were fine silk, and all of them were white.
He fell into his bed as if there was no more
  strength in his body, and at once began to snore
  like a sea lion. Now when Judith saw him there,
  she said to Abra, "Walk ahead of me; take care,
be slow and quiet; you must guard the door for me!"
  They stayed with Holofernes, just where they had to be,
  awake and watchful, Abra silent at the door,
  alert for guards and servants, but they were sleeping, for
they'd had so much to drink, and were so overfed
  that every single one was sleeping like the dead.
  That's the fate of people who drink hard and overstuff:
  they can't keep watch, or guard, as they're not alert enough.,
He who is King of Heaven, and can work His will,
  chose to rescue His people and kept the sleepers still.
  Judith approached the bed, and closer crept, to part
  the curtains wide, and with a wildly beating heart,
she joined her hands together, raising them on high,
  and on her knees, tearfully, addressed the sky:
  "O Lord, let me obey Your will: move me to do,
  as Your handmaiden, what I know will best please You.
Give me strength and courage to act right now, I pray.
  Be merciful to me and help me put away
  all fear, and reach my goal. Guide and make strong my hand,
  that all may fear You, Lord, and do as You command!
And liberate, I beg You, holy Jerusalem—
  Your city—and Your people in it—rescue them!
  Bring down the arrogant who fancy themselves great;
  the humble, virtuous ones, protect and elevate.
Lend me the power to do what I believe is right,
  and if it's necessary, help me with Your might
  that I may spend my life—devote my nights and days—

to obeying Your commands, and rendering You praise!"
Then, rising from her knees, square-shouldered, straight and tall,
    silently drew the sword. While one hand gathered all
    of Holofernes' hair, the other drew the blade
    across his neck. Blood spurted from the wound she made.
Groaning, he shuddered, face up in the bed where he was lying,
    arm and leg both twitching, throat bleeding, and then dying.
    So Holofernes died, who was a mighty lord,
    bitten by a tiny worm, a woman, with his sword,
A female conqueror it was who gave his boast the lie:
    he vowed to conquer the whole world; instead he had to die.
    He thought not even God could match his mighty power,
    but one small worm defeated him when it was his hour.
He lay there like a fallen log, that wretch, stretched out,
    because God favored Judith when she faced that lout,
    so that she would not falter but achieve her end.
    Then Judith stood beside the corpse and told her friend,
"Here, Abra, take and hide this in our sack!" and tossed her way
    the head of Holofernes, the prey she bagged that day.
    She stood up straight and pulled the cover from the bed
    wrapping the corpse, then off to pray, as local custom said.
They crossed the courtyard quickly, as if headed to prayer;
    Though sweaty, took no rest, as when the hawk is there
    soaring above, guarding the peak, clenching the prey
    meant for her hungry chicks, because she knows that they
await the food they need, which she was pledged to bring
    into the woven nest that shelters her offspring.
    Just so these women, both, without any rest, run,
    knowing that their people want freedom, and have none.
At last they see the guardians, watchful on the wall:
    they climb up the embankment, where they are heard by all.
    Judith stopped and raised her hand and shouted with pride,
    "Open the fortress gates! The Lord is on our side!
Open, open, for God, infinite in His powers,
    aided His people with His might, for He is ours!
    He to the faithless only punishment has given,
    casting them down: but unto us, he brings the grace of heaven!"

Translated from the Croatian by Rhina P. Espaillat with Henry R. Cooper, Jr.

MICHELANGELO BUONARROTI (1475–1564) was an Italian sculptor, painter, architect and poet. He was born in Caprese, near Arezzo, and grew up in Florence. He spent much of his later life in Rome, where many of his most famous sculptures and paintings, including the Sistine Chapel, were completed.

83

What in your handsome face I see, my lord,
　I'm hard put to find words for, here below.
　Often it lofts my soul to God, although
　wearing, that soul, the body like a shroud.
And if the stupid, balefully staring crowd
　mocks others for feelings after its own fashion,
　no matter. I'm no less thankful for a passion
　pulsing with love—faith, honor in accord.
There's a Fountain of Mercy brought our souls to being
　which all earth's beauty must in part resemble
　(lesser things, less) for an eye alert to truth.
No other hint of heaven's here for our seeing,
　hence, he that a love for you sets all a-tremble
　already hovers in heaven, transcending death.

106

From heaven it ventured forth, there must return,
    the immortal soul. To your flesh, its lifetime jail,
    an angel of mercy it came, to countervail
    our tainted thought, show fit respect for earth.
My love's aflame only for this, whose worth
    is beyond your classic beauty that takes the eye.
    For what else, in this spawning hubbub born to die,
    can a love all truth and honor hope to yearn?
That's how with all things noble, new-created,
    that nature lavished her care on, heaven too
    rifled its treasures for. Thanks be, that where
in the main God shows His glory, it's radiated
    veiled in some mortal form it shimmers through.
    And it's such I love, for the beauty mirrored there.

274

Oh let me see You everywhere I go!
    If mortal beauty sets the soul afire,
    Your dazzle will show how dim it is; desire
    for You burns high, as once in heaven's own air.
It's You alone, my dearest Lord, my prayer
    appeals to against passion's futile anguish;
    only You can give me vision to distinguish
    what I should think, wish, do, though slack and slow.
You tethered me to time, no road-to-bliss way,
    sentenced, though stooped and faint, to endless ranging,
    shackled in heavy flesh, remissions few.
What can I do to escape from living this way?
    Your power divine is my one chance of changing.
    I've nothing to fall back on, Lord, but You.

285

So now it's over, my day's long voyage, through
　　tumultuous ocean, in a hull unsteady;
　　　I've come to the world's last anchorage, and make ready
　　life's log with its every reckoning, foul and fair.
The daft illusion once so cuddled there
　　that art was a sovereign lord to idolize,
　　　I've come to know—how well!—was a pack of lies,
　　such as, to their grief, men treasure yet as true.
Fond, foolish, the lovesick longings felt before,
　　what becomes of them, my double death approaching?
　　　One certain-sure, one muttering harsh alarms.
Painting and sculpture soothe the soul no more,
　　its focus fixed on the love divine, outstretching
　　　on the cross, to enfold us closer, open arms.

288

The world and all its fables long ago
　　took over my time for contemplating God.
　　　Grace?—I dismissed it with a careless nod,
　　sinning worse than if I'd had a chance at none.
What made some wise made me a witless one,
　　blind to the way I'd straggled off awry.
　　　Now hope's gone dead, and many a time I sigh
　　to be disengaged from the self I touted so.
Shorten the road that heavenward winds and rises,
　　though shortened, dearest Lord, by half again
　　　I'll need your steadying gesture's admonition.
Teach me disdain of all the mad earth prizes,
　　beauties I love and made so much of then,
　　　for eternal life is now life's sole ambition.

290

Rid of this nagging nattering cadaver,
  dear Lord, and tattered all my bonds with earth,
  like one worn out, a sprung old skiff, I'd berth
  back in your halcyon cove, foul weather done.
The thorns, the spikes, the wounded palms each one,
  your mild and kindly all-forgiving face,
  promise me full repentance, thanks to grace
  rained on my somber soul—and reprieve forever.
Don't judge with justice as your holy eyes,
  and your ear, as pure as dawn, review my past;
  don't let your long arm, hovering, fix and harden.
Let your blood be enough to purge for Paradise
  my sump of sin, and, as I age, flow fast
  and faster yet with indulgence, total pardon.

293

Burdened with years and crapulous with sin,
  bad habits ruggedly rooted, no control,
  I see impend two deaths, of body, of soul,
  but am feeding my heart on poison none the less.
For myself, no strength I can muster in distress
  is enough to change my ways, life, love, or fate,
  unless You show the road, Who illuminate
  with your *do* or *don't* the muddlement we're in.
Not enough! Not enough, dear Lord, that You give the wish
  to set my sights heaven-high. Wish won't insure
  that my soul, next time from nothing, is made anew.
Before You undress it quite of its threads of flesh,
  cut half from the high steep trek I now endure,
  so I'll have heaven's destination full in view.

296

If our very thirst for longer life bids fair
  to promise my many years yet even more,
  that doesn't mean death's not huddling at the door
  or, seeing me unconcerned, holds off a while.
Why want more life for enjoyment's sake? Exile,
  grief, desolation—that's where the Lord's adored.
  But high on the hog long years—what's underscored
  by the but: the merrier, the more mischief there.
If, thanks to your grace, sometimes, my dearest Lord,
  zeal in its fiery impulse storms the heart,
  encouraging comfort and trust—doubt in suspension—
since no resources I dare call mine afford
  such élan, that's when my heaven-bound thrust should start.
  The longer we lag, the less our good intention.

298

With no less joy than grief and consternation
  that You, not they, were the victim doomed to die,
  the chosen souls saw great gates in the sky
  swing wide—Your blood the key—for mortals here.
Their joy: in seeing Your creature in the clear
  after primal guilt and its aftermath of loss;
  their grief: aghast at Your agony on the cross,
  a servant of servants and true love's oblation.
Who You were, come from where, heaven lavished clues:
  all its bright eyes went dim, rock bottom split,
  the mountains shuddered, and pitch-black the sea.
He raised the elders from their glum venues,
  found for lost angels a more dolorous pit.
  Only man, at His font reborn, sang jubilee.

Translated from the Italian by John Frederick Nims

MARTIN LUTHER (1483–1546) was a German priest, monk, theologian, translator and hymn writer. He was born in Eisleben and grew up in Mansfeld. He was educated at the University of Wittenberg, where he remained as professor for the rest of his life. He is widely considered the central figure in the Protestant Reformation.

A MIGHTY FORTRESS IS OUR GOD

A mighty fortress is our God,
A bulwark never failing;
Our helper He, amid the flood
Of mortal ills prevailing.
For still our ancient foe
Does seek to work us woe;
His craft and power are great,
And armed with cruel hate,
On earth is not his equal.

Did we in our own strength confide,
Our striving would be losing,
Were not the right Man on our side,
The Man of God's own choosing.
You ask who that may be?
Christ Jesus, it is he;
Lord Sabaoth his name,
From age to age the same;
And he must win the battle.

And though this world, with devils filled,
Should threaten to undo us,
We will not fear, for God has willed
His truth to triumph through us.
The Prince of Darkness grim,—
We tremble not for him;
His rage we can endure,
For lo! his doom is sure;—
One little word shall fell him.

That Word above all earthly powers—
No thanks to them—abideth;
The Spirit and the gifts are ours
Through him who with us sideth.
Let goods and kindred go,
This mortal life also;
The body they may kill:
God's truth abideth still;
His kingdom is forever!

Translated from the German by Frederic H. Hedge

VITTORIA COLONNA (1492–1547) was an Italian noblewoman and poet. She was born in Marino, near Rome, and grew up on the island of Ischia, near Naples. She married a brilliant military commander, whom she rarely saw. After his death, she moved to Rome, where she became friends with Michelangelo and advocated for a more Protestant view of salvation within the Catholic Church.

I

All the while my widowed love
flushed me with thoughts of literary fame,
it fed a serpent in my breast
and now, afflicted, languishing,
my only remedy is God.
                              From now on,
let the sweet nails be my quills,
his blood my ink, my text
his scored and sacred body.
No more Parnassus, no more Delos:
I must labour over other mountains,
other seas.
                    And pray to the sun,
which lights up earth and sky,
that he will loose his shining spring,
pour me water equal to my thirst.

3 I

If this little music, stirring the frail air,
can gather up the spirit,
open it and melt it as it does—
If this mere breeze of sound, this mortal voice,
can lift the heart so,
heal it, startling thought and firing our resolve—
what will that heart do when,
before God in the first and ancient heaven,
it hears the music of all being?
When, struck by truth, it steps forth
in the great wind of that singing?

4 I

When to the one he most loved, Jesus
opened what was in his heart,
when he spoke of the betrayal, the plot
that was to come, it broke
the heart inside his friend. In silence—
for the others must not know—
the tears cut gutters in his face.
                            But seeing this,
his master held him to his breast,
and before the ditch of pain
had closed inside, had closed his eyes
in sleep.
            No eagle ever flew as high
as the divine one in the moment of that falling.
This was God, who was himself alone,
both light and mirror. His rest
true rest, his sleep
true sleep, and peace.

56

We are blind. The ancient fear of death
assails us often, for we do not carry on our backs
the great and solid wings of hope.
Nor do we build our houses on that rock,
but dig in sand
and call our losses cruel. Yet death
is what makes room for love.
May I not hoard the mortal beauty
that surrounds me. May I learn to see instead
how, in the fire of being, suffering
is turned to light.

79

I would be lying, o sweet comfort, if I said
it's not the time or place to act upon this fervour,
the desire I bear within me, brightly lit.
But if I seem distracted, if I fail
in the attention I would always give, know this:
my heart is firm; your grace inspires it;
I will not set my sail to any other port.
You've helped me understand that pain and disappointment
cannot turn the wise man from his path.
The only thing that really slows our progress
is self-love, a weakened faith
in what is high, holy, invisible.

103

I am afraid the knot in which for years
my soul has been bound up now rules: I write
from habit, not because I am on fire.
I am afraid the knot is tightly tied,
and by myself: I'm proud
and therefore dull. I think
my days are useful
when in fact I waste them.
Come, then, flame of love:
sear me from within
again. Make me make my song
from silence and hoarse cries.
God listens only for my heart.
He cares nothing for my style.

Translated from the Italian by Jan Zwicky

PIERRE DE RONSARD (1524–1585) was a French Catholic poet. He was born into a noble family at Couture-sur-Loir in central France and was educated at the Collège de Navarre in Paris. His deafness kept him from pursuing a serious career, but he took minor orders in the church. He was the leader of the Pléiade, a prominent group of poets which also included Joachim Du Bellay.

FROM *CHRISTIAN HERCULES*

But where then is the eye, however blind,
Where is the soul, however misaligned,
That, should it care to understand my meaning,
I can't make hear by reasonably explaining:
For all they write of Hercules, by rights
Most of it's solely due to Jesus Christ?

So first, what were those three nights Jupiter
Suspended to make only one appear,
When he desired Alcmene in his grasp,
But that number of years that had to pass
For Jesus to receive a mother's birth,
So great the mystery heaven brought forth
Before He hid his Godhead's power away
Beneath the cloak of our humanity?

And what's the tale of Juno, murderess,
Delivering to the crib of Alcides
Two giant snakes to kill him where he lay,
If not King Herod, who, to do away
With the child Jesus, sent out through the land
Of Bethlehem his warlord high command
To kill both him and any little child
They found who had not lived to two years old?
Both were considered to be sons of men,

Like us, pure human, of the common strain,
Named by the people to be simply sons,
This, Joseph's child, and that, Amphitryon's,
Though Jesus took his being from God, whereas
It's Jupiter who authored Hercules.

And later, what were those venomous monsters,
Those Dragons Hercules confronts and masters:
A thousand terrors, a thousand beasts so weird,
That dreadful snake with seven heads that reared,
That Lion, those Centaurs that he forced to yield,
Geryon, Busiris and Cacus he killed,
Live monsters all, grotesque belligerents—
If not the vice and overwhelming sins
That Jesus Christ by his celestial force
In dying put to death on his great cross?

And what was she, Hesione of Troy,
Chained to a rock, staked out there as the prey
For a sea monster, and Prometheus
Strung up for eagles in the Caucasus,
Both of whom Alcides freed from their torture,
Unbinding them, if not our human nature
(Adam, I mean), whom Christ in goodness loosed
Out of the bonds that his own sin had fused,
When, like an unrelenting eagle, Law
Grasped at his soul, poor sinner, with its claw—
Hopeless, till by the faith of Christ, His Grace
Took on the Law and put it in its place?

And what was Hercules, subject forever
To Eurystheus, if not Christ to His Father,
Fulfilling His will to His final breath,
His humble servant to the point of death?

And what was Juno in her jealousy,
Who hated, held in constant enmity
All Alcides accomplished in this world,

But Satan, who endlessly hatched and hurled
His rage against Christ's glory, trying in vain
To spoil the victory his cross had won?
And what was that, when Hercules restrained
With one hand the God Pluto, when he came
To wrestle him on dead Alcestis' tomb,
And made him send her back to life and home,
But Jesus, who stopped death dead and exerted
His power then, when he resuscitated
Beloved Lazarus, from depths of night
Re-naturalised into this world of light?

And what was that, when Hercules renounced
His old wife so that he could be pronounced
The husband of a conquest newly made,
But Jesus, who declined the offered bride,
The older Church of the first Jews, and chose
Instead the Gentiles' church to be his spouse?

As Hercules took his wife's shirt to wear,
So Jesus Christ did something similar,
Assuming the human integument
Of that Church He loved, loved to the extent
He met for her the cruel death he bore,
As then hers were the garments that he wore.

Translated from the French by Clive Lawrence

We Must Forsake Homes, Orchards and Gardens

We must forsake homes, orchards and gardens,
  the vases and vessels carved by artisans,
  and chant our obsequies in the way of a swan
  who hymns his demise along Meander's banks.
Finished, I have run out my destiny's spool
  and lived to make my name famous enough.
  My pen flies to heaven to become a star,
  far from worldly charms that tempt even the best.
Happy who never was; happier who returns
  to the void from which he came; happiest
  who dwells, an angel newmade, with Jesus Christ,
leaving his robe of clay to fester below
  which was fate, fortune and destiny's toy,
  from the body's ties free to be spirit alone.

                    Translated from the French by Burl Horniachek

Luís de Camões (c. 1524/1525–1580) was a Portuguese soldier, official and poet. He was born into a prominent family from Alenquer, just north of Lisbon, and attended the University of Coimbra. He served as a Portuguese soldier and administrator in India and China, and survived a shipwreck off the coast of Cambodia. After completing his national epic *The Lusiads*, he returned to Lisbon, where he died in poverty.

O Glorious Cross

O glorious cross, O victorious
   and holy prize that encompasses everything;
   O chosen miraculous sign ordained to bring
   your remedy to each and every one of us.
O living font of sacred blood, expel
   our sins and cure our sinful souls. In You,
   O Lord, we know the almighty God, who
   embodies the gentle name of mercy as well.
With You, the time of vengeance ends. A new
   compassion flowers forth, forever and ever,
   like after winter, when springtime blossoms again.
So vanquish all your enemies, Lord, You
   who've made so many changes, yet never
   cease to be exactly what You've always been.

EXILE

Here in this Babylon, that's festering
　　forth as much evil as the rest of the earth;
　　Here where true Love deprecates his worth,
　　as his powerful mother pollutes everything.
Here where evil is refined and good is cursed,
　　and tyranny, not honor, has its way;
　　Here where the Monarchy, in disarray,
　　blindly attempts to mislead God, and worse.
Here in this labyrinth, where Royalty,
　　willingly, chooses to succumb
　　before the Gates of Greed and Infamy;
Here in this murky chaos and delirium,
　　I carry out my tragic destiny,
　　but never will I forget you, Jerusalem!

REFUGE

You who seek serenity in the wide
　　tempestuous sea of the world, cease
　　and abandon all hope of ever finding peace,
　　except in Jesus Christ, God Crucified.
If wealth absorbs your thoughts and preoccupies
　　your nights, God is the greatest treasure of all;
　　And if you're looking for beauty, always recall
　　that God alone is the Beauty that satisfies.
If you seek delights to set your heart on fire,
　　remember that God's the sweetest of all, Who rewards
　　His followers with victory at last;
If honor and glory are what you most desire,
　　no greater honor or glory has ever surpassed
　　humbly serving the highest Lord of Lords.

BELIEF

Truth, Love, Reason, and Merit can touch
    every soul and make it firm and strong,
    but Time, Luck, Chance, and Fate have long
    ruled over this world that troubles us so much.
Our thoughts contain a thousand things, yet we're resigned
    to never know their cause. And though we crave
    to know what lies beyond this life and the grave,
    we know it's inaccessible to the human mind.
Lofty speculations have been conceived
    by philosophers, yet experience is always preferred,
    since seeing always seems better and more precise.
Yet so many things that *have* happened are not believed,
    and so many things are believed that *never* occurred . . .
    So the best of all is to believe in Jesus Christ.

THE PASSION

So why has the triune God, in agony,
    sacrificed Himself for the insane sin
    of Man? Because no man could ever begin
    to withstand the just and heavy penalty.
Who could endure the necessary pains?
    Who could suffer such injury, death, and disgrace?
    No one, except for God, whose sovereign grace
    commands, and reigns, and obeys, as He ordains.
The resources of men are way too weak and small;
    they could never sustain the pain of God's just plan
    for righteous and necessary restitution.
So God's great strength endures it all,
    with a pure and merciful love for helpless Man:
    who makes the error, but never the retribution.

THE VIRGIN MARY

To fall in love with his whole world, his own
    creation, God made you, most holy Mary,
    a purest virgin so extraordinary
    that God retained you for himself alone.
In his holy Mind, he conceived you, his paradigm,
    long before Genesis, and long before Eve.
    So we praise your singularity and believe
    your essence was planned at the beginning of time.
I know that I could never, on my own,
    fully express the holy qualities
    created in you, who bore his perfect Son.
You're Daughter, Mother, and Wife. And if you alone
    have exalted these three awesome dignities,
    it's because you've delighted the Three-And-Only-One.

INCARNATION

Descending from heaven, our most benign,
    great God incarnated the Blessed Virgin. But why
    did God descend to the human? To sanctify
    all men, so they could aspire to the divine.
But why was he born so helpless and poor—to begin
    His life under the tyrant, Herod? To prepare
    the way for his sacrificial death, to bear
    the penalties of Adam's foolish sin.
But Why? It was Adam and Eve who broke God's laws,
    eating the forbidden fruits so long ago?
    Yes, they tried to be "like gods" despite God's plan.
And that's why God became human? Yes, because,
    in His mercy, He decided that, although
    men wished to be gods, God would become Man.

NATIVITY SCENE

The greatest beauty descends from heaven to earth,
   uniting itself to our flesh and making it great
   and noble. Once, it was humanity's fate
   to be poor, but today it's exalted by His birth.
The richest Lord of all is satisfied
   with the greatest poverty, sanctifying
   his love for the world: a tender infant lying
   in the straw, putting the glories of heaven aside.
Why did God come to earth so destitute?
   Because he is content with what is poor,
   since poverty is both precious and provident.
His birth, representing such absolute
   destitution, reveals to us: that the more
   the poverty, the more He is content.

SERMON

How, blind sinner, can you, so thoughtlessly,
   commit these dreadful evils, always repeating
   yourself, when you know that life is but a fleeting
   moment in time compared with all eternity?
Never imagine that God, our Judge, will suspend
   His laws and excuse your sins without their fair
   just punishment—or that your day of despair
   and reckoning will be slow to come. Don't spend
another hour, or day, or month, or year
   befriending evils that will, in time, create
   further damage and further retribution.
Since you know the truth of your errors, fear
   them all, put them aside, and capitulate:
   begging for God's mercy and absolution.

Translated from the Portuguese by William Baer

Fray Luis de León (1527–1591) was a Spanish friar, theologian, translator, Biblical scholar and poet. He was born in Belmonte, Cuenca, south-east of Madrid, and was educated at the Universities of Salamanca, Toledo and Alcalá. He became a professor at the University of Salamanca, but was imprisoned for four years for allegedly heretical opinions, before being cleared and returning to teach.

On the Ascension

Do you leave, shepherd saint,
your flock here in this valley, deep, obscure,
in loneliness and plaint,
and rise piercing the pure
high air—to that immortal refuge sure?

Those who were formerly
lucky are melancholy and grieving too.
You nourished them. Suddenly
they are deprived of you.
Where can they go? What can they now turn to?

What can those eyes regard
(which one time saw the beauty of your face)
that is not sadly scarred?
After your lips' sweet grace
what can they hear that isn't blunt and base?

And this tumultuous sea,
who can hold it in check? Who can abort
the gale's wild energy?
If you're a sealed report,
then what North Star will guide our ship to port?

O cloud, you envy us
even brief joy! What pleasure do you find
  fleeing, impetuous?
  How rich and unconfined
you go! How poor you leave us and how blind!

To Francisco de Salinas, Professor of Music at the University of Salamanca

The air becomes serene
and robed in beauty and an unknown light,
  Salinas, when the unseen
  deep music soars in flight,
governed by your hand that is wise and right.

  Before that holy song
my soul, submerged in its oblivion,
  recovers sense and long
  forgotten memory in
its dazzling and primordial origin.

  And having knowledge of
itself, it comes alive in thought and fate,
  and has contempt, above
  all, for mere gold, the bait
of blinds mobs, or beauty in its false state.

  Piercing the air, the soul
reaches into the very highest sphere
  and there it hears a whol-
  ly different mode: imper-
ishable music, first and without peer.

  It sees the way the grand
master works the immense zither, and the way
  he shapes the holy strand
  of sound with dextrous play,
by which that deathless temple is sustained.

It is composed, then, by
concordant numbers that accompany
   a consonant reply,
   and both work stubbornly
to mingle lost in sweetest harmony.

   Here the soul sails around
inside a sea of sweetness, and finally wheels
   about and then is drowned
   so that it hears or feels
nothing that foreign accident reveals.

   O happy deep collapse!
O death conferring life! O sweet oblivion!
   Now let me never lapse
   into the low, vile run
of senses! Let my rest in you be won!

   I call you to this good
joy, you the glory of Apollo's holy
   choir, friends whom I could
love beyond all wholly
vain wealth, for all the visible is sad folly.

   O Salinas, let me hear
the music of your fingers as it rings
   constantly in my ear,
   my senses wakening
to holy grace and dulled to earthly things!

Translated from the Spanish by Willis Barnstone

JAN KOCHANOWSKI (1530–1584) was Polish poet and courtier. He was born in Sycyna, near Radom in the south of Poland. He studied at Königsberg and Padua, before returning to Poland to serve at court. He later retired to the countryside, where he married and had seven children, including his daughter Ursula, who died at age two and for whom he wrote his Laments.

LAMENT 19, OR: A DREAM

Through the long night, grief kept me wide awake;
My body was worn out, my mind all ache
And restlessness. The dark was growing pale
Before sleep touched my brow with its black veil.
Then, at that instant (was I lulled by charms?),
I saw my mother, holding in her arms
My Ursula, my never lovelier
Daughter, in white nightgown, gold-curled hair,
Rose-petal skin, eyes bright as a new day—
Just like those mornings when she'd come to say
Her prayers for me. I stared and stared, until
My mother spoke: 'Are you asleep, or ill
With sorrow, son?' At which, my own deep sigh
Seemed to have wakened me; but presently
She spoke again: 'Your cry! Your cry, my dear,
Disturbed my distant shore and brought me here;
Each moan of yours, each bitter tear you shed
Has reached the hidden chambers of the dead.
Here is your girl: look at her smiling face
And be consoled. Take heart. Although your case
Is hard in the extreme, although you are
In torment, mind and body, every hour,
Be comforted. Why make yourself heartsick?
Why is your mind a burning candlewick
Wasting itself? You think the dead are gone,
Extinct forever, banished from the sun?

You are mistaken: there, the lives we live
Are far more glorious. There we are alive
Beyond the flesh. The dust returns to dust,
But spirit is divine, a gift that must
Return to its Giver. Trust and understand
This mystery: she sits at God's right hand.
You cannot see her as she is—your sight
Is mortal and sees things in mortal light—
But now your daughter shines, a morning star
Among angelic spirits. You who are
So desolate, know that she prays for you
And for her mother—as she used to do
When she was still a child learning to speak.
To you her life may have seemed short and bleak,
She may have missed the pleasures adults know—
But what are pleasures when they end in woe?
The more you have, the faster your life moves
Towards the loss of it. Your own case proves
This beyond doubt. Your daughter brought you joy
But could that match the pangs that now destroy
All your tranquility? It never could,
So recollect yourself. This desolate mood
Is natural when your child is in the grave,
But how would she be better off alive?
What did she lose? Not true peace or delight.
She freed herself from things that devastate
Our life on earth with heartbreak and despair,
Things that weigh down the cross that humans bear
And haunt their moments of felicity
With deep foreboding and anxiety.
So why do you keep crying? My God, son,
What is there to regret? That no man won
Her dowry and her heart, then made her years
One long declension into strife and tears?
That her body wasn't torn by labour pains?
That her experience was, is and remains
Virginal, that she got release before
She learned if birth or death mark women more?

Earthly boundaries limit earthly joys—
Heavenly joys are boundless. Paradise
Exists forever, crystalline, secure.
There happiness is absolute and pure;
There tragedy, disease, death have no place;
There tears are wiped away from every face.
We live our endless lives in endless bliss.
We know the cause of each thing that exists.
Our Sun will never set; our days don't end,
The dark and fear of night never descend
Upon our realm, where we unceasingly
Witness our Maker in His majesty.
You mortals cannot see Him. Still, dear son,
Turn your thoughts toward Him, try to live on
Consoled by changeless heaven's certainty.
You've learned how futile earthly love can be,
Heed now the other, heavenly love's voice!
The truth is: your girl made a better choice.
Thus, sailors making for the open sea
Will head back towards the haven when they see
Dark clouds above; while others, who keep going,
Are wrecked on blind reefs when the gale starts blowing
And drowned and lost; lucky the few who are
Cast up on shore safe, clinging to some spar!
Had she outlived the Sibyl, her one fate
Would still be death. So why prolong that wait
For what was certain anyhow? She chose
Departure over waiting, chose to close
The door early and cut life's sorrows short.
Some lose their parents and have no resort
But orphanages; some are married off
In haste and lose their fortune and young life
To God knows what impostor; others still,
Abducted and made slaves of, tread the mill
In some wild heathen enclave, stooped and lame,
Praying for death to come and end their shame.
These threats are threats your child no longer faces.
Her life on earth was happy, an oasis

Of small protected joys, a heaven-sent
Interlude, short-lived but innocent.
It was for her, my son, things turned out best,
So dry your tears. Believe. Take comfort. Rest.
Weigh up your losses, ponder each mistake,
Yet never overlook what is at stake:
Your peace of mind, your equanimity!
However robbed of these you seem to be,
However little of a help they are
Be your own master. Every evil star
Shines with impunity and as of right:
No matter how it hurts, we must abide,
We must obey. That burden's placed upon
Each one of us, so why then feel, my son,
You have been singled out? She was mortal too,
And lived as long as she was destined to.
You think not long enough? But even so,
You cannot alter it, and who can know
How living on for just a few more hours
Would have been better? The Lord's ways are not ours.
Our task is simply to accord with them.
Tears cannot call back souls who are called home.
For how can we on earth adjudicate
Fairly upon what seems unfair in fate?
Prone to see things in the worst light, mankind
Can hardly recognize or bear in mind
The fortunate things. And yet proud Fortune's ways
Are not to be contested. Sing in praise
Of loss even, in praise of all that's left
That might have gone instead down Death's dark shaft.
You must accept, although your wound's still raw,
The rule and sway of universal law
And fill your heart with new peace, banish pain:
Whatever is not loss should be called gain.
What profit have you reaped for all that cost,
That foolishly, irretrievably lost
Time you spent poring over books, those years
Of study that still leave you in arrears?

By now your grafting should have yielded fruit:
Windfalls of wisdom, comfort, resolute
Self-mastery. When others were in pain,
You've helped them over it, time and again;
Now, master, you will have to heal yourself.
Time is the cure for everything, but if
Somebody has such faith in his own power
Of healing, should he wait another hour?
Yet what is time's great remedy? The wax
And wane of things, and nothing more; the flux
Of new events, now painful, now serene;
He who has grasped this accepts what has been
And what will be with equal steadfastness,
Resigned to suffer, glad to suffer less.
Bear humanly the human lot. There is—
Never forget—one Lord of blight and bliss.'
She vanished, and I woke, uncertain what
I had just seen: was this a dream or not?

Translated from the Polish by Seamus Heaney and Stanislaw Baranczak

ST. JOHN OF THE CROSS (1542–1591) was a Spanish priest, friar, mystic and poet. He was born into a Jewish *converso* family in Fontiveros, near Ávila. He grew up in poverty and studied at the University of Salamanca under Fray Luis de León. Along with St. Teresa of Ávila, he led a controversial effort to reform the Carmelite Order, for which he was imprisoned. After escaping, he continued to work for reform until his death.

THE DARK NIGHT OF THE SOUL

One darkest night I went,
aflame with love's devouring eager burning—
O delirious event!—
no witnesses discerning,
the house now still from which my steps were turning.

Hidden by darkness, bent
on flight, disguised, down secret steps sojourning—
O delirious event!
Hidden by dark, and yearning,
the house now still from which my steps were turning;

In that most blissful night,
in secrecy, since none had seen my going,
nor did I pause for sight,
nor had I light, for showing
the route, but that which in my heart was glowing.

This only did the guiding,
surer than the blaze when noonday shone,
to where he was abiding—
who was to me well known—
where we would be together and alone.

O night that led me true,
O night more fair than morning's earliest shining,
O night that wrought from two—
lover, beloved entwining—
beloved and lover one in their combining!

On my new-flowered breast,
to him alone and wholly sanctified,
he leaned and lay at rest;
his pleasure was my guide,
and cedars to the wind their scent supplied.

Down from the tower, breezes
came, while soft fingers winnowed through his hair;
a touch that wounds and pleases
caressed my throat with air,
leaving every sense suspended there.

I stayed, all else forgetting,
inclined toward the beloved, face to face;
all motion halted, letting
care vanish with no trace,
forgotten in the lilies of that place.

I Went In, I Knew Not Where

I went in, I knew not where
and stayed, not knowing, but going
past the boundaries of knowing.

I knew not the place around me,
how I came there or where from,
but seeing where then I found me,
I sensed great things, and grew dumb—
since no words for them would come—
lacking all knowledge, but going
past the boundaries of knowing.

Of piety and of peace
I had perfect comprehension;
solitude without surcease
showed the straight way, whose intention—
too secret for me to mention—
left me stammering, but going
past the boundaries of knowing.

So wholly rapt, so astonished
was I, from myself divided,
that my very senses vanished
and left me there unprovided
with knowledge, my spirit guided
by learning unlearned, and going
past the boundaries of knowing.

He who reaches that place truly
wills himself from self to perish;
all he lately knew, seen newly,
seems trifles unfit to cherish;
his new knowledge grows to flourish
so that he lingers there, going
past the boundaries of knowing.

The higher up one is lifted,
the less one perceives by sight
how the darkest cloud has drifted
to elucidate the night;
He who knows the dark aright
endures forever, by going
past the boundaries of knowing.

This wisdom, wise by unknowing,
wields a power so complete
that the learned wise men throwing
wisdom against it compete
with a force none can defeat,
since their wisdom makes no showing
past the boundaries of knowing.

There is virtue so commanding
in this high knowledge that wit,
human skill and understanding
cannot hope to rival it
in one who knows how to pit
against self his selfless going
past the boundaries of knowing.

And if you should care to learn
what this mode of being wise is,
it is yearnings that discern
the Divine in all its guises,
whose merciful gift and prize is
to confound all knowledge, going
past the boundaries of knowing.

SONG OF THE SOUL THAT TAKES PLEASURE IN KNOWING GOD BY FAITH

How well I know the spring that feeds the torrent,
though night has fallen!

The spring runs from forever, and past finding;
how well I know it as it flows down winding,
though night has fallen.

Since it has none, I know not where its source is,
but know that there all things begin their courses,
though night has fallen.

I know nowhere exists so fair a treasure,
yet heaven and earth there slake their thirst with pleasure,
though night has fallen.

So clear it shines that nothing foul can scum it,
and every light, I know, emanates from it,
though night has fallen.

So full its current, and so strongly churning,
that heaven rains on hell and on the burning,
though night has fallen.

The stream that flows, I know, from that first welling
equals the source in might beyond all telling,
though night has fallen.

The stream that from these two flows forth together
keeps equal pace, as bonded by a tether,
though night has fallen.

For that eternal spring is safely hidden
in this, life's bread, the feast to which we're bidden,
though night has fallen.

They're called to this, all creatures here abiding,
to come and drink their fill, although in hiding,
since night has fallen.

That living fountain that I most desire
I find in this, the bread of life, entire,
though night has fallen.

GLOSA: TO THE DIVINE

The beauty that can be eyed
will never be my undoing,
but rather what, beyond viewing,
only fortune can provide.

The taste of what can't endure
does no more, when it's diminished
desire, than make impure
the palate, whose joys are finished;
sweets whose sweet cannot abide
will never be my undoing,
but rather what, beyond viewing,
only fortune can provide.

160

A generous heart disdains
to loiter where travel's restful:
it prefers to take the stressful
route, where, beset by pains,
it will not be turned aside
from its undeterred pursuing
of what it knows, without viewing,
only fortune can provide.

He who knows the pain of love
by the divine hand ignited
finds himself no more delighted
by tastes he has wearied of,
as the sick man, satisfied
with no mess of potage stewing,
hungers for what, beyond viewing,
only fortune can provide.

Do not find it strange to learn
such a taste can so persever;
so unlike all else whatever
is the food for which you yearn
that all creatures far and wide
are torn from themselves with ruing
the lack of what, beyond viewing,
only fortune can provide.

For if once the will has known
the touch of the true divine,
for nothing less can it pine
than divinity alone.
Such beauty cannot be spied
but by faith itself, close hewing
to delights that, beyond viewing,
only fortune can provide.

Tell me, then, how such a lover
should not give you grief to bear,
since no substance does he wear
no form or feature for cover
of all who on earth reside,
kinship and support eschewing,
seeking for what, beyond viewing,
only fortune can provide.

Do not believe that the core,
whose value is so much higher,
finds the joy that lights desire
in what here we hunger for:
present beauty and, beside,
past and future, all accruing
is less than what, beyond viewing,
only fortune can provide.

Better does he swell his hoard
who labors for future reaping,
than one more busy with heaping
harvest he has lately stored.
Therefore to be magnified
I am ever up and doing,
to gain the prize beyond viewing
only fortune can provide.

Which is why I take my stand
that what our senses perceive
as beauty "though we believe
it fair and pronounce it grand"
the beauty that can be eyed
will never be my undoing,
but rather what, beyond viewing,
only fortune can provide.

Translated from the Spanish by Rhina P. Espaillat

TORQUATO TASSO (1544-1595) was an Italian poet and courtier. He was born in Sorrento near Naples, and studied at Padua and Bologna. He entered the service of the ruling family in Ferrara and there completed *Jerusalem Delivered*, an epic on the First Crusade. He began to show signs of madness and was eventually confined. After release, he traveled from court to court throughout Italy until his death.

JERUSALEM DELIVERED

From Canto 9

[After devils begin to fight against the Franks, God sends the archangel
Michael to stop them.]

55
And the French are already in retreat
when Guelph and his band arrive in the nick of time,
and make them turn about and take the brunt
of the mad fury of those men of crime.
And so they battled, and the streams of blood
flowed the same on both sides. But the sublime
Monarch of heaven meanwhile from His throne
turned His eyes towards the battle. He alone,

56
there seated, deals to all the universe
good and just Law, creates the orders bright
over the limits of the narrow world.
Reason and sense cannot attain that height;
and from august eternity He shines
in three illuminations of one light,
His servants Fate and Nature at His feet,
and Motion too, and Time which measures it,

163

57
and Place, and She who as a breath or wisp
scatters and turns (as it is willed up there)
the glory and power and gold we find on earth.
We scorn her, but the goddess does not care.
He robes Himself in His resplendent light
which even the blessedest visions cannot bear;
round Him immortal spirits numberless,
unequal in their equal happiness.

58
To the great chorus of the joyful hymns
resound the happy realms of heavenly light.
He summons Michael, he whose warlike arms
are all of burning adamant flashing bright,
"See how that evil crew of Hades arms
against my faithful flock and my delight,
rising out of the deepest pit of hell
to vex the world, to kill my people! Tell

59
"that swinish legion they should leave the care
of fighting wars to warriors, as is best—
No longer to infect and cloud the air,
the land of the living, or the shores of the blest—
and return to the night of Acheron, there
to suffer justice in their proper nest,
to lash themselves and souls in the abyss.
I have commanded, I have fated this."

60
Then the chief of the winged hosts who fight
bowed reverently before the feet of God.
He spreads his golden plumes for the great flight
with a swiftness surpassing thought,
and passes the empyreal fire and light,
the changeless glory where the blest are brought,
and sees the crystalline sphere in pure perfection,
the star-gemmed sphere that whirls in the other direction,

61

then to the left sees Jove and Saturn turning.
diverse in look and in the roles they play,
and the miscalled "planets" (if angelic virtue
moves and informs them, they can never stray);
then leaves the region where it rains and thunders,
the flaming fields of everlasting day,
to come to our world in its constant strife
of self-destruction, feeding, death, birth, life.

62

He shook the smoke from off his ageless wings
and the thick gloom that round about him rolled,
and his face scattered gleams and glistenings
of heavenly light that touched the night with gold.
So after a rain the sun, cloud-hidden, flings
its bow, and all its lovely hues unfold;
so cleaving the midnight's calm and liquid rest
a star will fall to the great mother's breast.

63

Arriving where the wicked crew of hell
stoked up the fury of the pagan band,
he hovered in the air on his strong wings
and shook his spear, and had them understand,
"You above all by now should know quite well
with what a horrifying flash the grand
King of the Universe thunders—who deride
the cruelest pain and misery in your pride.

64

"The Lord has sworn that Sion's walls will bow
unto the Cross, and open its gates again.
Why rouse the wrath of the celestial court?
Why battle fate? What can you have to gain?
Go then, accurst, to your own punishment,
your realm of everlasting death and pain—
and let those dungeons you have merited be
where you fight and parade in victory.

65

"There whet your cruelty to its utmost strength
against the wicked, there amid their aching
cries through eternity, the gnashing teeth,
the dismal clank of iron, the chains shaking."
So he, and if they were laggards leaving, with
his fatal lance he jabbed them on. Forsaking
the golden stars and the lovely realm of light,
they moaned, and toward the abyss they turned their flight,

66

their flight to the abyss, to make the pain
of sinners bitterer then usual—
so huge a flock never flapped over the main
when the days first grow warm and comfortable,
nor ever have so many dry leaves lain
on the ground in the first hard frost of Fall.
Everything looks less black when these depart;
set free from them at last, the earth takes heart.

From Canto 13

*[In the midst of a drought, Godfrey of Bouillon, the leader of the Franks,
   prays for rain to revive his troops.]*

70

Godfrey too heard and saw it, but abhorred
what would have been the quickest remedy.
and with the faith that made the rivers stand
and mountains hurl themselves into the sea,
he prayed devoutly to the King of the world
to open His springs of grace and clemency;
he clasps his hands, zeal burning in his breast,
and turns his eyes toward heaven with this request:

71

"Father and Lord, Who rained down the sweet dew
of manna in the desert for Your flock,
Who gave a mortal hand the power to
strike living water from the riven rock,
now let us see these wondrous signs anew,
and if our merit fail us, our poor stock
replenish with Your grace, Who are the source.
Help us, for we are called Your warriors."

72

His supplications are not slow to move
for from a meek and just desire they rise,
and swift and light they fly to heaven above
like feathered angels, to the Lord most wise
Who takes them up; and with a father's love
unto His faithful hosts He turns His eyes,
and moved with pity for all they hazarded
and all their labors undergone, He said,

73

"The tide has gone against the host I love,
suffering in their fight with the infidel,
enduring the secret arts and weapons of
the legions of the whole world, and of hell,
till now. For the new order now begins,
prosperity returns, and all is well.
Let it rain; bring the banished warrior home,
And, for his fame, let Egypt's armies come."

74

With that He bent His brow, and the vast heavens
trembled, and every fixed and wandering light,
and the reverence-stricken air and the plains of the sea,
and the hills and blind Hades felt His might,
and they heard the thunder boom out of the west
and saw prophetic lightning flashing bright,
and to the flashes and the roars on high
the men sent up a loud and joyful cry.

75

Behold the clouds at once, not of this world,
not gathered to the skies by the sun's power,
but from the open gates of heaven hurled
they come down in a vast and sudden glower—
and in the shadow of night the day is furled,
and all the land grows dark in one brief hour,
and the rain slashes down and makes such head
it sets the stream to spilling from its bed.

76

As sometimes in the hottest days of summer
when the skies shower down the wished-for rain,
a flock of noisy ducks on the muddy river
will wait for it and happily complain,
and quack and ruff their wings for the cold water,
and take a bath—for none of them refrain,
but where the water's deepest they swim first
and all go bottoms-up and quench their thirst,

77

with such a happy shout the soldiers hail
the rain sent down by heaven's merciful power,
and the men to soak their shirts strip off the mail
or let their hair be drenched in the cool shower;
some use the helmet for a drinking pail,
some dip hands in the stream and let it pour,
some splash it on their temples, in their faces,
while shrewder folks collect it in their basins.

78

Their hearts were gladdened, they were strong again—
nor were the men the only ones restored,
for the earth had suffered too, a dry, bare plain
whose stricken members were all cracked and scored
with fissures. Now she took the swelling rain
into her deepest veins, and ministered
unto all things above the moisture's powers,
nourishing all the trees and grass and flowers,

168

79

as if, parched with a fever to the quick,
she'd been refreshed by a life-giving juice,
and, throwing off the cause that made her sick,
that fed upon her substance, now broke loose
like a new springtime with her flowers strewn thick
and reawakened greenery, profuse—
so now forgetting all her past duress
she reassumes her garlands and glad dress.

80

At last the rain was over, and the sun
returned, but with a sweet and temperate ray,
full of the masculine power that warms the earth
at the end of April, or in early May.
O noble faith! Who honors God aright
can sweep the pestilential air away
and change the seasons' order, or their state,
defeating the anger of the stars, and fate.

Translated from the Italian by Anthony M. Esolen

GUILLAUME DE SALLUSTE DU BARTAS (1544–1590) was a French Huguenot courtier and poet. He was born into a family of wealthy merchants from Gascony in south-west France. He studied law in Toulouse and served as a judge in Montfort. Later, he entered the service of the Protestant nobleman Henri de Navarre, but died before Henri converted to Catholicism and became king.

THE WEEK, OR THE CREATION OF THE WORLD

From The Seventh Day

God is the soul, the life, the strength, the sinew
That quickens, moves, and makes this frame continue.
God's the mainspring that maketh every way
All the small wheels of this great engine play.
God's the strong Atlas, whose unshrinking shoulders
Have been and are heaven's heavy globe's upholders.

God makes the fountains run continually,
The days the nights succeed unceasingly;
The seasons in their season He doth bring,
Summer and autumn, winter and the spring;
God makes earth fruitful, and He makes the earth's
Large loins not yet faint for so many births.
God makes the sun and stars (though wondrous hot,)
That yet their heat themselves inflameth not,
And that their sparkling beams prevent not so
With woeful flames the last great day of woe.
And that, as moved with a contrary wrest,
They turn at once both north and east and west.
Heaven's constant course His heat doth never break;
The floating water waiteth at His beck;
Air's at His call, the fire at His command,
The earth is His, and there is nothing fand

In all these kingdoms, but is moved each hour
With secret touch of His eternal power.

God is the judge who keeps continual sessions
In every place, to punish all transgressions;
Who, void of ignorance and avarice,
Not won with bribes, nor wrested with device,
Sans fear or favor, hate or partial zeal,
Pronounceth judgments that are past appeal.
Himself is witness, judge and jury too,
Well knowing what we all speak, think or do,
He sounds the deepest of the doublest heart,
Searcheth the reins, and sifteth every part.
He sees all secrets, and His lynx-like eye,
Ere it be thought, doth every thought descry.
His sentence given never returns in vain;
For all the heaven, earth, air and sea contain
Serve Him as sergeants, and the winged legions
That soar above the bright, star-spangled regions,
Are ever pressed for powerful ministers,
And lastly for His executioners.
Satan, assisted with th'infernal band,
Stands ready still to finish His command.

God, to be brief, is a good Artisan
That to His purpose aptly manage can
Good or bad tools; and for just punishment
He arms our sins us sinners to torment;
And to prevent th'ungodly's plot, sometime
He makes His foes, will-nill they, fight for Him.

* * *

He would this Sabbath should a figure be
Of the blest Sabbath of eternity;
But th'one, as legal, heeds but outward things,
Th'other to rest both soul and body brings,
Th'one but a day endures; the other's date

Eternity shall not exterminate.
Shadows the one, th'other doth truth include;
This stands in freedom, that in servitude;
With cloudy cares th'one's muffled up some whiles;
The other's face is full of pleasing smiles.
For never grief, nor fear of any fit
Of the least care shall dare come near to it.
'Tis the grand jubilee, the feast of feasts,
Sabbath of Sabbaths, endless rest of rests,
Which with the prophets and apostles zealous,
The constant martyrs and our Christian fellows,
God's faithful servants and His chosen sheep,
In heaven we hope within short time to keep.

He would this day our soul, sequestered
From busy thoughts of worldly cares, should read
In heaven's bowed arches, and the elements,
His boundless bounty, power and providence,
That every part may, as a master, teach
Th'illiterate, rules past a vulgar reach.

Come, reader, sit, come sit thee down by me;
Think with my thoughts, and see what I do see.
Hear this dumb doctor; study in this book,
Where day and night thou may'st at pleasure look;
And thereby learn uprightly how to live;
For every part doth special lessons give,
Even from the gilt studs of the firmament
To the base center of our element.

Seest thou those stars we wrongly "wandering" call?
Through divers ways they dance about this ball,
Yet evermore their manifold career
Follows the course of the first-moving sphere.
This teacheth thee that, though thine own desires
Be opposite to what Heaven's will requires,
Thou must still strive to follow, all thy days,
God, the first Mover, in His holy ways.

Vain puff of wind, whom vaunting pride bewitches
For body's beauty or mind's richer riches;
The moon, whose splendor from her brother springs,
May by example make thee veil thy wings;
For thou, no less than the pale Queen of Night
Borrow'st all thy goodness from the Prince of Light.

Wilt thou from orb to orb, to earth descend?
Behold the fire which God did round extend;
As, near to heaven, the same is clear and pure,
Ours here below, sad, smoky and obscure,
So while thy soul doth with the heavens converse,
It's sure and safe from every thought perverse;
And though thou won here in this world of sin,
Thou art as happy as heaven's angels bin.
But if thy mind be always fixed, all,
On the foul dunghill of this darksome vale,
It will partake in the contagious smells
Of th'unclean house wherein it droops and dwells.
If envious Fortune be thy bitter foe,
And day and night do toss thee to and fro,
Remember, th'air corrupteth soon, except
With sundry winds it be oft swindled and swept.

The sea, which sometimes down to hell is driven
And sometimes heaves a frothy mount to heaven,
Yet never breaks the bounds of her precinct
Wherein the Lord her boisterous arms hath linked,
Instructeth thee that neither tyrant's rage,
Ambition's winds, nor golden vassalage
Of avarice, nor any love, nor fear
From God's command should make thee shrink a hair.

The earth, which never all at once doth move,
Though her rich orb received from above
No firmer base, her burden to sustent,
Than slippery props of softest element,
By her example doth propose to thee
A needful lesson of true constancy.

Nay, there is naught in our dear mother found
But pithily some virtue doth propound.
O let the noble, wise, rich, valiant,
Be as the base, poor, faint and ignorant;
And looking on the fields when Autumn shears,
There let them learn, among the bearded ears,
Which still the fuller of the flowery grain,
Bow down the more their humble heads again,
And ay the lighter and the less their store,
They lift aloft their chaffy crests the more . . .

Thou, thou that prancest after honor's prize,
While by the way thy strength and stomach dies,
Remember honor is like cinnamon,
Which nature mounds with many a million
Of thorny pricks, that none may dangerless
Approach the plant; much less the fruit possess.

Canst thou the secret sympathy behold
Betwixt the bright sun and the marigold,
And not consider that we must no less
Follow in life the sun of righteousness?

O earth, the treasures of thy hollow breast
Are no' less fruitful teachers than the rest;
For, as the lime doth burn and break in water,
And swell and smoke, crackle and skip and scatter,
Waking that fire whose dull heat sleeping was
Under the cold crust of a chalky mass;
He that, to march amid the Christian host,
Yields his heart's kingdom to the Holy Ghost,
And for brave service under Christ his banner
Looks to be crowned with his Chief Champion's honor,
Must in affliction wake his zeal, which oft
In calmer times sleeps too securely soft.

And opposite, as the rich diamond
The fire and steel both stoutly doth withstand,
So the true Christian should, till life expire,
Contemn proud tyrants' raging sword and fire.
Or if fell rigor with some ruthless smart
A little shake the sinews of his heart,
He must be like the richest mineral,
Whose ingots bend but never break at all,
Nor in thy furnace suffer any loss
Of weight but lees, not of the gold, but dross.

The precious stone that bears the rainbow's name
Receives the bright face of Sol's burnished flame,
And by reflection, after, it displays
On the next object all those pointed rays;
So whoso hath from the empyreal pole,
Within the center of his happy soul
Received from splendor of the beams divine,
Must to his neighbor make the same to shine;
Not burying talents which our God hath given
To be employed in a rich trade for Heaven,
That, in his church, he may receive his gold
With thirty, sixty and an hundred fold.

As iron, touched by th'adamant's effect,
To the north pole doth ever point direct,
So the soul, touched by the secret power
Of a true, lively faith, looks every hour
To the bright lamp which serves for cynosure
To all that sail upon the sea obscure.

Translated from the French by Josuah Sylvester

MIKOŁAJ SĘP SZARZYŃSKI (c. 1550–c. 1581) was a Polish poet. He was born near Lvov and educated at the universities of Wittenberg and Leipzig. For a short time, he was sympathetic to Protestantism, but later became an ardent Catholic. He probably died in south-eastern Poland.

TO THE HOLY VIRGIN

O Lady without any equal, the other
    Adornment of mankind, in whom humility
    Spoiled not the heart nor glory spoiled humility,
    Of your Creator the mysterious Mother!
O you, who came the cruel serpent to destroy
    When the entire world was poisoned with its venom,
    You have risen to heaven above the kingdom
    Of angels, in your glory you possess pure joy.
You are like the true moon of our souls, in whose glow
    We can see the beams of eternal mercy
    When our terrible sinfulness relentlessly
Brings upon us sad night and its heavy shadow.
    But you, be the coming of morning's dawn, summon
    And reveal to us the desired light of your sun.

ON THE WAR WE WAGE AGAINST SATAN, THE WORLD, AND THE BODY

Peace—is happiness, but earth's condition
   Is struggle. The stern Hetman of darkness
   And the world's sweet vanities are tireless
   As they persevere for our corruption.
O most powerful Lord, if this were all!
   Our house for passing pleasures—the Body—
   Envying the spirit's authority
   Continues always to covet our fall.
In such fearful combat what shall I do,
   Weak and divided within, unheeding?
   The one true peace, O universal King,
The hope of my salvation lies in You!
   Put me by Your side, then I will safely
   Wage war, and win a lasting victory!

Translated from the Polish by John and Bogdana Carpenter

VITSENTZOS KORNAROS (1553–1613/1614) was a Cretan poet and government official. He was born in the village of Sitia, but, after his marriage, moved to the capital Candia (present-day Heraklion). He was the author of the long romance poem *Erotokritos* and a leading figure in the Cretan Renaissance. He is also thought by many scholars to have written the anonymously published sacred drama *The Sacrifice of Abraham*.

FROM *THE SACRIFICE OF ABRAHAM*

SARAH:
I don't have strength left anymore, and all my power fails me
This is what tribulations bring, a suffering that ails me
Right in the gut; I am so dizzy that my knees give way.
I do not have the mind to beg the Lord; I cannot pray.

ABRAHAM:
Beloved wife, don't carry on as if you were a child.
That which we suffer is the will of God; be reconciled.
Come close and sit beside me, do not weep, do not lament it;
The tears and beating of your breast, poor dear, will not prevent it.
The child we had was not our gift, a favor for our sake,
But the Creator favored us; what He gives He can take.
What do you want, ill-fated one, with tears you weep in vain?
You torture me, a wretch myself, and nothing is to gain.
O Sarah, daughter, this is not the hour for lamentation;
It is a day for patience, and a time of consolation.

SARAH:
(O woe and suffering—o frightful mystery, o power—
When people tell me, child, that you have turned into a flower.)
And you—how will you nerve yourself for slaughter, for the killing
Of such a blameless body—won't you freeze and be unwilling?
And do you want your vision to go black, the light abhor you,
As you behold your dying child when he expires before you?

How will you have the strength of heart to listen to his cries,
When like a lamb his body twists and turns before your eyes?
And you, o heedful child, where are you headed, do you know?
To what place do they summon you? Down what road do you go?
As for your father and your mother, how long will we wait
For your return—what week, what month, what season, or what date?
And O my heart with all its trembling leaves, will not it quake,
To hear another child called by your name—my heart will break.
My child, how will I bear to be apart from you, how hear
The voice of someone else, and not the one I hold most dear?
My child, is it because you wanted to desert your mother
You turned out so obedient, more so than any other?
As long as I shall live, my son, I never will allow
Another boy to speak to me—this is a solemn vow—
My eyes will be cast down upon the earth and never stray,
And so forever I'll recall the message of this day.

ABRAHAM:
Sarah, don't heap more toil and suffering on my heart, don't rave
And make me as dishonored in my old age as a slave,
Don't frighten me from my resolve, so that I hesitate,
And use the weapon on myself and meet an evil fate.
Gather your wits, amend your errors, for the things you say,
These utterances, do not please the Lord in any way.
Who is it you oppose? Why does your weeping never rest?
Why is it that you question God's commands and his behest?
Our child, our bodies, souls, well-being, all are God's alone;
It all belongs to the Creator, nothing is our own.
Just let God shed his grace, as I set off upon the path
Of sacrifice—and may my offering appease his wrath.
I do not want to linger any longer, nor delay.
I'll wake the child and get him up and then be on my way.

SARAH:
Nine months I carried you, my cargo, dearest child, who'd nestle
Inside my body, this unlucky hull, this darkened vessel.
For three years, son, I gave you milk from my breasts, day and night,
For you, who were my very eyes, who were my very light!
I watched you as you grew—how like a tree's branch grew apace—

And you increased in virtue, and in wisdom, and in grace.
Now tell me child what joy you plan to give to me, I wonder—
When you'll be lost and melt away, like lightning or like thunder.
And as for me, how will I live without you, all bereft?
What courage will I have in age, what freshness will be left?
When God announced to us, to both together, man and wife,
You would be born to us, what joy that brought into our life.
O wretched House of Abraham! What happiness the birth
Of you, my child, was brought to it when you appeared on earth.
How do such joys turn into sorrows in a single day?
How do the good things scatter, like a cloud that blows away?

ABRAHAM:
Let us not dwell upon these things when he's destined to die.
What help is it to him, what good is it to cry and cry?
You only weary God, who takes no joy in our fulfilling
The oath and sacrifice, because he sees we are unwilling.
Banish these sighs, banish this bitterness that's so distressing—
Let us give thanks to our Creator, source of every blessing.

SARAH:
Go then, my husband, since it is the will of God, and may
The path before you be all milk and honey on the way.
Go, and may the Lord have mercy, may he lend an ear,
And on the mountain may there be sweet news today to hear.
I'll say I never bore him, never saw him, for no doubt
I held a burning candle in my hands and it went out.

ABRAHAM:
Come now, don't wallow in your bitterness, hasten to dress him,
And kiss him on the lips, and bidding him farewell, caress him,
Dress him to set out on the journey, quickly get him ready,
And may He who commands it give you peace and keep you steady.

SARAH:
Here is the light I looked on, the sweet life that will bereave me,
These are the eyes that the Creator won't ordain to leave me.
Here is the burning candle you are planning to extinguish,

180

This is the body whose destruction you will not relinquish.
He lies there like a little lamb, he's sleeping like a bird,
He fusses in his sleep about his father's heartless word.
Look at the child, the poor, sweet child, and tell me, have you ever
Laid eyes upon a child so pale and drained of color?—never.
Behold the child's humility, his face before your eyes—
It is as if he hears and witnesses his own demise.
My darling son, do you see bitter dreams? And is that why
You lie hunched up, and in your sleep you whimper and you cry?
Last night when I put you to bed, you were all full of joy,
And my own heart was happier than ever, dearest boy.
And as you fell asleep, my dear, I stood watch at your side,
I watched you with delight and happiness, giddy with pride.
You drifted into sleep as you were playing with your mother,
And I found myself happy, happier than any other.
And now why do you go?, and for what reason are you leaving
Me blind in darkness, in a world of suffering and grieving?

ABRAHAM:
Don't let your tears reveal to him a mystery so dire—
The dreadful revelation's shock might cause him to expire.
But gently, gently wake the lad instead, and do not cry,
And get him dressed with tenderness, and bid the boy goodbye.

SARAH:
What sort of face, what sort of heart is able to conceal it,
A mystery so dreadful, as in no way to reveal it?
Wake up, my precious, dearly reared, for whom we gave our best,
And go now to the feast, where you're invited as a guest.
Now dress, put on your travelling clothes, the finest from the loom,
And follow, not your father, lord and master, but your doom.
O child, o heedful child, accept the blessings that I send,
The ending of your life will bring my own life to its end.
May blessings upon blessings, good son, on your journey find you,
My blessings on your footsteps, both before you and behind you.

ABRAHAM:
Hush, Sarah, do not cry, and do not speak, I beg you—face
That you must let us go, and leave. Give us a little space.
Do not wake up the child with all your words of bitter meaning,
But make your heart as iron, let there be an end of keening.

SARAH:
I will be silent, Abraham, if you will let me wake him
And dress and make the poor boy look his best before you take him:
He is invited down to Hades for a wedding feast,
Let him be so arrayed that none may fault him in the least.

Translated from the Greek by A.E. Stallings

Bálint Balassi (1554–1594) was a Hungarian soldier and poet. He was born at Zólyom in the Kingdom of Hungary (present-day Zvolen, Slovakia). He was raised as a Protestant, but later converted to Catholicism after a disastrous marriage. He died at the siege of Esztergom-Víziváros from a leg wound caused by a cannonball.

To Merciful God, That He Might Condescend to Protect Him in His Hiding and that He Might Extend Further Grace unto Him

Merciful deity,
unto whose charity
my life is delivered:
Of burdens relieve me,
guide me and lead me,
now friendships are severed.

Straight from my infancy
thou hast been all to me,
mentor and saviour:
I like a child to thee,
following timidly,
fretting for favour.

My poor hopes steadfastly
from childhood exclusively
in you are invested.
Trusting, I leant on you,
gave my assent to you,
on you have I rested.

What would it profit you
to cast my soul off if you
leave me in danger,
who am saved by thy son,
and thy son have become,
no longer a stranger?

Hear as I pray to thee,
for sake of thy name to me,
great name of power;
Show me beneficence,
blessed inheritance,
in this my good hour.

Reward me according to
hopes that I've stored in you
for my tomorrows;
Let me be blessed by thee,
I who did trust to thee,
bear thou my sorrows.

The dew that anointeth
the springtime buds pointeth
to grace ever verdant;
Therefore anoint me,
to favour appoint me,
thy long faithful servant,

That my heart may cherish
thy joys till I perish,
still singing thy praises,
Thy great name, creator
than all the world greater,
live thou in my phrases.

These words of devotion
beside the great Ocean
I endite for thy reading,
In the year ninety one
half millennium on
from the thousand preceding.

GRANT ME TRANQUILITY

Grant me tranquility,
calm impassivity,
heavenly Lord!
Guard my poor sanity,
my heart in captivity,
put to the sword!

Through long years of penitence,
my spirit craved sustenance,
desiring salvation;
Shield me and watch with me,
let not your enmity
cause my damnation.

Not without labour
you saved me, my saviour,
through death of your son.
For his sake assist me
that you might complete
what you had begun.

Your mercies so mighty,
not my sins unsightly,
should precedence have,
Your grace is eternal,
though my sins infernal
cry out for the grave.

Can you in beatitude
suffer vicissitude
or loss of possession?
Can you awaken
the ranks of forsaken
by thy intercession?

Why should I doubt,
when despair is cast out
in trust of your word;
Freely you'll grant me
the grace not denied me,
the faithful's reward.

Lord, do not resist me,
unclench your great fist,
be tender and kind,
Forgive my beginnings
and heal the torn wings
of my pitiful mind.

Flying, I'd bless you,
adoring address you,
my trespass defying,
Thus practiced in flight,
my soul being healed might
I rise in my dying.

Translated from the Hungarian by George Szirtes

Luis de Góngora (1561–1627) was a Spanish priest and poet. He was born into a noble family in Córdoba, but lived most of his life in Valladolid and Madrid. After his health began to fail, he retired to Córdoba, where he died in poverty.

On the Nativity of Christ Our Lord

Hung from the Cross, pierced by a lance in the side,
    both temples punctured with a crown of thorns,
    to offer such mortal suffering in exchange
    for our salvation, that was indeed a deed;
yet greater still to be born in want, as proof
    how far for us you'll stoop, how far you'll travel,
    born where there's no lodging but a stable,
    where a simple porch must serve, without a roof.
It was not the greater deed, O my great Lord,
    to overcome time's brutal, chill offensive,
    opposing it in weakness with a strong breast
(as to sweat blood is more than suffering cold),
    because there is a distance more immense
    between God and man than between man and death.

Translated from the Spanish by John Dent-Young

Lope de Vega (1562–1635) was a Spanish playwright, sailor, priest and poet. He was born in Madrid into an undistinguished family and was educated at the University of Alcalá. He had several stints in the navy and was an extremely prolific writer. He had multiple wives, mistresses and children. In his later years, after much personal misfortune, he turned to the church and became a priest.

Tomorrow

Lord, what am I, that, with unceasing care,
    Thou didst seek after me, that thou didst wait,
    Wet with unhealthy dews, before my gate,
    And pass the gloomy nights of winter there?
Oh, strange delusion! that I did not greet
    Thy blest approach! and oh, to Heaven how lost,
    If my ingratitude's unkindly frost
    Has chilled the bleeding wounds upon thy feet!
How oft my guardian angel gently cried,
    "Soul, from thy casement look, and thou shalt see
    How he persists to knock and wait for thee!"
And, oh! how often to that voice of sorrow,
    "Tomorrow we will open," I replied,
    And when the morrow came I answered still, "Tomorrow."

The Good Shepherd

Shepherd! that with thine amorous, sylvan song
    Hast broken the slumber that encompassed me,
    That mad'st thy crook from the accursèd tree,
    On which thy powerful arms were stretched so long!
Lead me to mercy's ever-flowing fountains;
    For thou my shepherd, guard, and guide shall be;
    I will obey thy voice, and wait to see
    Thy feet all beautiful upon the mountains.
Hear, Shepherd! thou who for thy flock art dying,
    O, wash away these scarlet sins, for thou
    Rejoicest at the contrite sinner's vow.
O, wait! to thee my weary soul is crying,
    Wait for me! Yet why ask it, when I see,
    With feet nailed to the cross, thou 'rt waiting still for me!

Translated from the Spanish by Henry Wadsworth Longfellow

Tommaso Campanella (1568–1639) was an Italian friar, philosopher, theologian and poet. He was born in Stilo in Calabria, southern Italy, to a poor and illiterate cobbler. He was a child prodigy and entered the Dominican Order before the age of fourteen. He was often in trouble for his unorthodox views and spent twenty-seven years in prison for conspiring against the Spanish government in southern Italy. Among his other writings is the utopia *The City of the Sun*. After his release, he lived in France.

On the Metaphysical Highest Good

Song

Madrigal I

Being is the Highest Good, never lacking,
it needs nothing, and fears nothing.
All things love It always; but It only Itself,
because It has no betters, nor a peer more lovely.
If It is infinite, It sets us free in death,
since nothing can remain outside,
nor inside of It. Nor is anything ever
destroyed, but changes often.
The immense space of being
is the basis of everything, hidden in Itself,
that only rests in Itself,
from Which, by Which, and in Which all things are one;
and from Which each finite thing is very far
from the infinite; and because each is ingirded
and girded, each is also very close, remaining
alive in It and through It, though for us It is not distinct,
like rain in the sea never lacking.

Madrigal 2

Like space penetrates all beings
in their places, and likewise is penetrated by them,
so God internalizes beings, and space, and surpasses them,
not like a place, nor like the located thing,
but in a preeminent way. He imparts
the space to locational being, and mass to bodies,
and virtue to agents to be active,
and to composites, in which His Idea passes.
And because He is, consequently every being is, too;
like splendor from a candle;
but He hides and reveals Himself
in various guises in Whom all always live,
like atoms in the air. Into living flames
firewood resists change, and then delights
in being sparks. Love, virtue, and sense
of one's own being all leave their marks,
as much as necessary, according to their great Author.

Madrigal 3

Man was a baby, embryo, seed, and blood,
bread, plant, and other things, which he liked
to be when he was such, and disliked changing into
what he is now: and that which now worries him,
to be made fire, earth, mouse, or eel,
he will eventually like; and he will believe himself blessed
in what he will be, since in all beings shines
the divine idea, and then he will forget.
So nothing loves what it seems to love:
some suffer or do,
what its Being knows best to give it.
That one may be another, all resist. He who wants
to be duke, is, in as much as he is like one or produces
that image, whence he loves that; and he is not a duke, in as much
as he detests ruining himself to become duke. Then
there is yet another one, who is yet another one;
the wise one is all of them, while still not changed by death.

Madrigal 4

He did not make beings to live through them,
like a parent in children or a teacher in disciples;
nor to show another His grandeur,
since there was no other, and great architects
do not show to a flea their masterpiece,
nor does one seek honors who is not corrupted in oneself.
Now who will say why, if the eternal Intellect
does not tear away the veil of such arcane things?
If He always was, nothing never was;
and all beings are rays
of the First, in which I found
worlds, virtues, and ideas, within Him
made and remade in various guises *ab aeterno*,
new to the remade beings, made of ancient things;
figures and shadows of holy existences,
which in the First are one and harmonious,
despite how differing their appearances may be.

Madrigal 5

If fire were infinite, earth
would not be, nor would anything be similar or foreign.
If God is infinite good, one cannot say
that there is death or evil or Stygian lair,
except for the good of those whom He locks up.
By comparison, not in essence, is evil, as juniper
seems sweet to the goat, but bitter to us.
If such conditions are to have an end,
chaos alone will imbibe of every joy,
like iron receives
fire, and cold the snow.
And this is beautiful to the guiding virtue,
as it is beautiful that God's hand distinguish chaos.
What marvel is it if one kills oneself?
Fate guides him with hidden enchantments
along the great life where evils and madmen are
semitones and metaphors to His song.

Madrigal 6

God makes souls in their portable, dark,
closed tombs, doubtful about death,
ignorant of the future, and oblivious to the past.
Like many galley slaves and servants and thieves
I have seen who, despairing of a better life,
content themselves with prison, since they hate leaving it.
Now the soul, that resides in the opaque body,
is ignorant of itself, and other lives, and God;
whence through narrow holes, it faces and spies
what that soul really is,
and how and why it remains there.
The soul governs the body, and nourishes and guides it
with its rod; nor does it know in what way it calms and incites it,
since it does not shine through; and it is a brief light.
Thus he who works in the dark, does not see himself
nor his work; but at the balcony he learns
and sees, disputes, and revises himself in others.

Madrigal 7

If from plants and beasts human spirits
form well-adorned hostels in the dark,
and they maintain them with an art unknown to them,
it is necessary that you, God, Who sojourn in them,
guide them, and that their beings are, to obey You,
like the pen does the writer: the pen is blind, but takes note;
or like the body is to the soul, and the souls to the Prime
Being, without Whom not one iota is made.
Being, power, knowledge, love, and making are
passions in us and a gift,
and actions in God, Who is good.
Loving and sensing Himself, He loves and senses
all things that in Him are known.
He enjoys their comedy, since the celebration
is made inside Him; and He does not take joy away from them;
but, rejoicing, gives it back to them, and lends
sense and love, while He loves and understands Himself.

Madrigal 8

But we, finite beings, actually in prisons, take
what is outside of us, from that which batters our walls,
where through narrow passages only a little false knowledge
enters, from which you, false loves, are born.
Thus air, earth, and sun we believe are dead,
at least those who are free to perceive, not the dead, like us;
and yet we love those who keep us in prison,
and wrongly hate those who refer us to Heaven.
Fate plays tricks on us to retain
our vital spirits,
as much as is necessary for its games.
Oh proud soul, rejoice, since one never dies!
The oblivion of old still makes you bitter.
Oh, blessed is the one who is free and has
the pure sense to judge all lives!
So, united to God, he goes securely
without fearing death nor Dis.

Madrigal 9

Song, we recognize, contrary to the impious,
the Author of the universe, confessing as
beautiful, good, and blessed all of His
works, in as much as they are His. The parts,
conditions, and fruits are to the Whole
so just that changing one atom alone
would turn all upside down. And He Who was, may He always be;
from Whom every being, I sense, is made
more content than it knows how to wish:
like everyone else we will speak in wonder, when
out of Lethe is opened that great sacrament.

Translated from the Italian by Sherry Roush

Francisco de Quevedo (1580–1645) was a Spanish nobleman, courtier, poet, novelist and prose satirist. He was born in Madrid and suffered from a club foot and severe myopia. He studied at the University of Alcalá and lived mostly in Valladolid and Madrid. He fell in and out of favor with the court, at times exiled from the capital or confined, and died shortly after his final release.

Well I See You Run, Swift Time

Well I see you run, swift time,
    A caulked ship on open sea;
    Or better still, like flight of bird
    Or arrow without track or trace.
Enduring in my wrongs, asleep,
    Dyed in strains, heavy with guilt;
    Though grief and plaint should cleanse and wash
    Me, still I bide my reckoning day.
I do not know when this shall come;
    I trust it's late, yet perhaps it's here;
    The sooner missed than believed.
Your breath, O Lord, make bold my will,
    Cleanse my soul, cure my wounded
    Heart, make soft my obdurate breast.

O LORD, THIS SOUL OF MINE A NEW

O Lord, this soul of mine a new
    Heart lacks, a new man needs; strip me
    Of myself, for it could be
    I paid your mercy what I owe.
I walk unsteadily the blind night,
    For I have come to loathe the day,
    And it's my fear to find cold death
    Enveloped in a mortal (though sweet) bait.
I'm your estate; your image,
    Father, I have been; if not your care,
    There's no thing else defends my cause.
Act as demanded by my ill faring,
    Not as I ask; for I'm so lost
    I hide rescue from my desire.

ADAM IN EDEN, YOU IN A GARDEN

Adam in Eden, You in a garden;
    He in all honour, You in your agony;
    He sleeps and his company ill-watches;
    You pray wide awake as yours slumbers.
His act was the first of disharmonies;
    You composed our primordial day;
    You drink the cup your Father sends;
    He eats defiance and lives as dead.
The sweat of his brow is his sustenance;
    That of yours is our glory:
    The guilt was his, the affront yours.
He bequeathed horror; You leave us a memory;
    His, a blind deceit; yours, a prime bargain.
    How different the story you leave us!

They Style Him King, Blindfold His Eyes

They style him King, blindfold his eyes;
    They want a seer who cannot see;
    A sceptre give, the wind will shake;
    A crown, of rushes and of thorns.
With scraps and trappings such as these
    Judea's kingdom wants its King:
    Who rules a reed, whom sorrow whelms
    And, blind, will suffer all its frets.
But the Lord, who justly sways the state
    With rod well-armed with iron-strength,
    A crowned compassion shows in love.
His battle buys his people peace,
    His sword and arrows strike himself;
    Lords of the earth, learn from Him.

Lelio, the Tears You Shed Dishonour

Lelio, the tears you shed dishonour
    The soft and copious sorrow, and
    With your easy plaint you slander
    The heart by yielding it to torment.
If you, brave man, love strict virtue,
    Let austere truth chastise feeling.
    Can you profanely call it punishment
    That God remembers you an instant?
A soul's strength is proved in grief;
    And human, eager toils burden
    But do not bend a noble neck.
The greater grief, the nearer God;
    God alone stands outside evil,
    And he who suffers stands above.

Translated from the Spanish by Michael Smith

Joost van den Vondel (1587–1679) was a Dutch poet and playwright. He was born in Cologne, Germany to a middle class Mennonite family from the Netherlands. His family moved frequently, until settling eventually in Amsterdam, where Vondel married and had children. He converted to Catholicism around 1641 and was a prolific writer. Many of his best plays were written in old age.

Lucifer

From Act 2

LUCIFER:
The Godhead's last decision, which the worth
Of Heaven rated less than that of Earth,
Oppresses us! Earth, in some puddle grown,
Is lifted to the stars, Man on the throne
Of angels set; we're robbed of our possession
And bidden slave and sweat at Man's discretion!
We Spirits, long assigned as Heaven's court—
Officials, are now called on to support
An earthworm, bred of matter and to serve it—
Worse, while it overshadows us, preserve it!
Why did the Source of Grace downgrade our state?
Some slothful Angel came on duty late?
How came the Godhead to select Mankind—
The nature of His chosen Angels find
Disposable? His life and soul inject
Into a body—birth and eternity connect—
Highest with lowest linking: God with Man?
Could anyone make sense of such a plan?
Shall now perpetual light succumb to night?
Shall I, Lieutenant of the Godhead's might,
To this unnatural being—this dwarf—kow-tow?
Unnumbered, fleshless, godlike Spirits bow

To such a creature—sinister and crude—
With God's own grace and majesty imbued?
Mystery too deep for Angelkind to measure!
You hold the key to the Almighty's treasure—
Resolve for us this hidden contradiction:
From Holy Writ, explain God's jurisdiction!

GABRIEL:
As far as I'm allowed to quote, I will . . .
But too much knowledge often serves one ill.
God lets us know what seems enough to Him:
Too bright a flash could blind the Seraphim!
True wisdom keeps its goal in part concealed,
While part disclosing. To obey and yield,
As Laws prescribe, befits a faithful servant,
At all times, of his master's will observant.
Reason and aim a mystery must remain,
While family-trees, unnumbered, wax and wane!
The Lord, who'll rule in time, as God and Man
Made one, and whose authority will span
The Earth, stars, oceans and all life we know,
Heaven hides from you. Why? . . . Time will show.
Meanwhile, obey! God's edict you have heard!

LUCIFER:
Why, then, it's true! This foreign earthworm's word
Shall here prevail and Heaven's Sons be faced
With alien domination, Man be placed
So high above our God?

GABRIEL:
                                    Accept your fate!
Your dignity's God-given, like your state.
Above all Angelkind, the Lord set you—
But not to grudge another glory due!
A rebel hazards crown and head the day
He flouts the Lord's commandments! Need I say,
Your brilliance stems from that of God alone?

LUCIFER:
I've bowed to none save God upon His Throne!

GABRIEL:
Then bow to God's decision! He made all
From nothing, all that lives or ever shall!
He steers all towards a goal beyond our knowing.

LUCIFER:
Exalting Man—God's light on him bestowing!
To see this Man, God-equal—and so soon,
Enthroned in clouds of incense, to the tune
Of umpteen thousand choirs intoning praise,
Drowning the majesty and diamond-rays
Of Day-Star, Lucifer—no longer shining—
While heavenly bliss gives way to sad repining!

GABRIEL:
True blessedness from calm content derives:
On glad acceptance of God's will, it thrives!

LUCIFER:
God's majesty is being severely slighted
If nature divine with human blood's united—
United and constrained! We Spirits, rather,
Approach God's nature, than do sons a father,
Bred by and like him. Is it not unfair,
Like with unlike in this way to ensnare—
Finite with infinite, power circumscribed
With boundless power? What if the Sun described
A faulty orbit, mantled itself in clouds
To light the world, or steamy shrouds
Of vapour black? No cause for joy on Earth!
Man's paltry glow would be of little worth!
Sun's progress robbed of all its majesty,
The heavens blind, the stars in jeopardy,
Order dispelled, legality expunged,
If once the source of light its brilliance plunged
Into a swamp! Forgive me, Gabriel!

You speak for the Almighty, I know well:
So, if I quibble or resistant seem,
Zeal to preserve God's rights and His esteem
Alone emboldens me thus far to stray
From pure obedience—

GABRIEL:
                              I'll not gainsay
Your valour in God's cause; but, bear in mind,
God's a far better judge than Angelkind
Of where His glory lies! In vain you look . . .
When God's made Man, shall He His secret book—
All seven seals—unlock, His secrets tell:
Taste then the nut, where now you bite the shell!
Then only, reason and cause—no longer guesses—
For all this secrecy we'll learn. The far recesses
Of Heaven's Holy of Holies we'll explore.
Till then, we must believe, respect, adore
In gratitude, till knowledge by its might,
Doubt overcomes, as daylight conquers night!
The Godhead's Wisdom, towards which, through the ages,
We reverently advance, enlightens us in stages
With scientific learning, but requires us,
Each at his post, to honour what inspires us:
Be first, my Lord Lieutenant, to comply!
I go where God ordains—
(Exit GABRIEL)

From Act 5

GABRIEL:
Infernal counsellors to left and right,
Lucifer then held forth, consumed with spite:
"You Powers, who in our righteous cause sustained
Grave injury, it's time revenge we gained
For all we've suffered! Heaven, let's persecute
With hate implacable and wiles astute . . .
God's chosen creature and the human clan
We'll smother in the crib, before they can

201

Grow strong enough their birthright to enjoy:
My aim is—Adam and his offspring to destroy!
By tempting Man, God's first command to flout,
A stain so deep that nought can wash it out,
I'll plant in Adam and his progeny,
So poisoning them, that they will never be
Admitted in our stead to Heaven's court—
Though just a few might, in the last resort,
To seize the Crown and State they covet, rise
Through travail, pain and death in varied guise.
Undreamt of ills shall spread in Adam's wake
Throughout the whole wide world! Nature shall quake,
Thrown out of balance, harmony destroyed,
Revert towards the Chaos of the Void!
I see Man, in God's image first created,
Forfeit that likeness and, alienated,
His will, imagination, wits grown dim—
Bereft of that inborn light God gave to him—
Loath, in his mother's pangs, to draw first breath,
Knowing he can't escape the jaws of death!
Ever more bold, I'll spread my rule of fear . . .
Henceforth, my sons, idols we shall revere,
From temple-altars in the sky extolled,
With offerings of livestock, incense, gold—
And humans so numerous, none could keep the score—
Mankind entire, condemned for evermore,
God's Name with deeds atrocious to besmear . . .
His victory and my Crown shall cost God dear!"

MICHAEL:
Accursed wretch! The Lord you still defy?
We'll bring you to your senses by and by!

GABRIEL:
Thus Lucifer spoke and sent Count Belial,
Without delay, to engineer Man's Fall!
Evil itself he donned, the guise of snake,
Subtlest of beasts. With honeyed words to make

202

The lure appeal to innocent Mankind,
His coils about the Tree of Knowledge twined.
"Did God on pain of death, free will deny?
Forbid you this—the sweetest fruit—to try?
No, surely, Eve—fair dove—you are confused!
I beg you, look upon this Apple, all suffused
With lustrous sheen of crimson and of gold.
A feast awaits you! Daughter, come, be bold!
No venom lurks in this immortal Tree . . .
Exquisite fruit! Taste it! I guarantee
Knowledge and Light you'll share. You shrink from sin?
Take it, if Glory and Wisdom you would win
To equal God's omniscient Majesty!
He may resent it—but that's how you'll see
That all things differ—nature, type and form."
At this, the young bride's heart began to warm
And she for this most precious fruit to yearn.
Her eye was charmed, then lips and mouth in turn
Her trembling hand, commanded by desire,
Did pluck and eat, with Adam: trespass dire
For all their offspring! Both at once enlightened,
Perceived their nakedness, then, shocked and frightened,
With fig-leaves clothed the shame of that first Sin.
They sought a shady wood to shelter in,
Striving in vain to cheat the All-seeing Eye.
The heavens frown . . . a rainbow spans the sky,
Which God's great wrath betokens and portends.
Angels bewail their fate, but no amends,
No wringing of hands, no pleas can save the pair.
The thunder crashes, lightning flashes flare!
They moan in terror, racked by misery;
They flee their shadows, but they cannot flee
The worm of guilt that gnaws through heart and head,
As, stumbling and staggering, they plunge ahead,
Both pale as death and blinded by their tears,
They see no light, no refuge from their fears,
Who lately walked in pride, with blameless poise,
Whom now a rustling leaf, the slightest noise,

Affrights. When, suddenly, a mighty cloud swoops low,
Splits open to emit a gleam—a glow—
Whence God appears and speaks with thunderous sound
That strikes the hapless couple to the ground.

CHORUS/MICHAEL:
Better had Man not seen the light of day,
Than for a bite of apple lose his way!

GABRIEL:
"O Adam," thunders God, "What means this flight?"
"Lord, I was naked, so I fled your sight!"
"Who told you nakedness was shameful?" God demands,
"You plucked forbidden fruit with sinful hands!"
"Alas, the Woman tempted me to eat!"
Said Eve: "The serpent lured me by deceit!"
Thus did they each attempt to shift the blame.

CHORUS/MICHAEL:
What sentence did God pass upon their shame?

GABRIEL:
Woman, who misled Man, by God's decree,
Shall suffer birth-pangs and Man's subject be;
While Man must toil and moil, must sweat and slave.
The earth he tills—and, in the end, his grave—
Thistle and thorn shall grow: the snake, meanwhile,
For having so misused its fork-tongued guile,
Shall on its belly creep and live on dust!
But, to give wretched Man firm grounds for trust,
God promised that, in future there should spring
From Woman's blood and Woman's seed, a King—
A Saviour, who should crush the Serpent's head
In enmity, through centuries unshed.
Although the snake the Saviour's heel may bite,
Yet shall He be victorious in the fight . . .

Translated from the Dutch by Noel Clark

MACIEJ KAZIMIERZ SARBIEWSKI (1595-1640) was a Polish poet, priest and scholar. He was born in Sarbiewo, north-west of Warsaw, in the Duchy of Masovia. He entered the Jesuits and studied at Vilnius, Polotsk and Rome. He returned to teach at Vilnius, before becoming court preacher to King Ladislaus IV in Warsaw.

BOOK IV. ODE XXVIII

Almighty Spirit! Thou that by
Set turns and changes from Thy high
And glorious throne dost here below
Rule all, and all things dost foreknow!
Can those blind plots we here discuss
Please Thee, as Thy wise counsels us?
When Thou Thy blessings here doth strow,
And pour on earth, we flock and flow,
With joyous strife and eager care,
Struggling which shall have the best share
In Thy rich gifts, just as we see
Children about nuts disagree.
Some that a crown have got and foil'd
Break it; another sees it spoil'd
Ere it is gotten. Thus the world
Is all to piecemeals cut, and hurl'd
By factious hands. It is a ball
Which Fate and force divide 'twixt all
The sons of men. But, O good God!
While these for dust fight, and a clod,
Grant that poor I may smile, and be
At rest and perfect peace with Thee!

Translated from the Latin by Henry Vaughan

ADAM MICHNA OF OTRADOVICE (c. 1600–1676) was a Czech Catholic poet, musician and nobleman. He was born in Jindřichův Hradec in Bohemia into a musical family. He became organist and choir director at the provost church there in 1633. He was married, but apparently had no children.

DISDAIN FOR THIS TRANSITORY WORLD

What avail is worldly glory?
Flesh like grass is transitory.
    Smoke we are, by rough winds carried,
    Here today, tomorrow buried.

What are royal throne and power,
Princely castle, knightly tower?
    All must come to dust and ashes:
    Death's last dance will end all passion.

What avail are youth and vigour,
Angel's face or fairest figure?
    E'en the rose must wilt and wither,
    Grave rots bone and skin together.

Be your eyes of crystal lightness,
Be your lips of coral brightness,
    Be your hair like red gold burning:
    Soon to clay it will be turning.

Rustling silk or golden treasure,
All which to the eye gives pleasure:
    Gold is sand, like sand you spend it:
    Vain the price that humans lend it.

What are crimson robe and ermine?
Merely blood and slime and vermin.
    Pride and riches will be humbled,
    Greatness mercilessly tumbled.

Ye who walk in velvet breeches:
Poverty the Master teaches!
    Silk is but the worm's extrusion,
    Worldly pride is but illusion.

What the silkworm has excreted,
Worthless, horrible and fetid,
    Man counts precious and entrancing:
    Silk he wears for feast and dancing.

So adieu, world of the senses,
Tempting me with vain pretences,
    Brief as smoke and flower vernal:
    I elect the joys eternal.

How the world behaves I care not,
In its vanity I share not:
    I am eager for salvation,
    Turn to pious meditation.

Translated from the Czech by Ewald Osers

PEDRO CALDERÓN DE LA BARCA (1600–1681) was a Spanish soldier, priest, poet and playwright. He was born in Madrid into a noble family and studied at the Colegio Imperial in Madrid and the University of Salamanca. He served in the army for over a decade, while also writing frequently for the theatre. In his latter years, he was ordained as a priest and wrote almost exclusively sacred dramas.

FROM *THE GREAT THEATRE OF THE WORLD*

WORLD:
First I will draw a black curtain across
To represent the turmoil of Chaos,
For it is best to hide away
Our set till we begin the play.
And then the mists shall disappear
And putting the vapours of darkness to flight,
Two lights shall shine out, bright and clear,
For there's no entertainment without light.
One is the golden lamp of day,
The other is that diamond
Upon the forehead of the night
Which casts a subtle silver ray.
The first act shown upon our stage
Shall represent a simple age
When Nature ruled life's gentle dawn.
And then, about the time that Time is born
A shining garden shall be shown
With burning colours and sweeping line—
Prodigies of natural design.

Branchfuls of blossoms, pink in the pink light,
Will open up, amazed by their first sight
Of the sun climbing up the sky.
The trees will yawn and stretch their roots

And they shall bear delicious fruits
Unpoisoned as yet by the serpent's lie.
A hundred crystal streams shall travel gaily
Over a thousand pebbles and flow on,
Meandering among the fields where, daily,
A million pearls sing in the Dawn.
Rolling meadows shall make this place
A heaven for the human race.
If hills and valleys are needed, you decide—
Hills and valleys shall be supplied.
The earth shall open up giant furrows,
I'll lay down rivers in all these sections
Which, like rabbits chased out of burrows,
Shall scoot off in all directions.

That was all Act One Scene One, but
As yet no building, house or hut
Has been observed upon the earth. But you
Wait for this – Act One Scene Two!
Flash! And I summon up cities and ports,
Palaces, temples, farms and forts.
And when the earth cries out for rest
From the weight of all this stone on her breast,
The entire stage I shall transform
To one almighty thunderstorm,
With avalanches of foaming mud,
Whirlwinds of hail and a great flood.

Then, through that pandemonium,
A curved ship with a roof shall come,
Lost on the trackless waters so
It trembles, not knowing where to go.
But safely down in its wooden womb,
Humans and animals shall find room.
And the sign of peace shall leap across the sky—
Red, orange, yellow, green and blue,
Indigo and violet shall shine through,
Ordering the army of the waves to dry.

And the great earth itself shall shake
Like a dog when it steps out of a lake.

The Law of Nature we call Act One
And now its distance has been run.
Director, let Act Two commence,
It's called the Law of the Commandments.
This act, as well as an excellent text,
Shall have spectacular effects,
For I shall unbutton the Red Sea's waves
And out of Egypt, her former slaves,
The Israelites, shall bravely tramp
Nor ever get their sandals damp.
Not only that, but every night
A pillar of fire I shall light.
Each day a cloud-pillar shall cross the sand
To lead them towards their Promised Land.

Moses in a swift cloud shall fly
To collect the Law from Mount Sinai.
And the second act shall be done
With a fierce eclipse of the sun
When the sun shall turn blood-red
And then go black and appear to be dead
And the skies shall be shattered, the mountains rumble,
The woods shall wither and the cities crumble
And after this frenzied act shall pass
There'll be nothing left but ruins and the grass.
Now the third act shall take place.
Act Three, which we call The Law of Grace.
The last act is the greatest one
And many miracles shall be done.

Act One: The Law of Nature.
Act Two: The Law of the Commandments.
Act Three: The Law of Grace.
And then we come to the end of the play
And the World will burn both night and day

So that, from a million miles away
The earth shall look like one flame, one pure ray.
I'm sorry, but when I think of that day,
My tongue dries up, what I feel I can't say.
My body shudders when I think of it.
My mind shakes when I imagine it.
I am astonished I can even say it . . .
I feel myself burning when I picture it.
Oh let this scene of pain and rage
Be postponed to some far distant age
And then postponed again, so people may
Never see their planet burned away!

* * *

BEGGAR:
This Beggar part, well I realise
That it seems right and proper in your eyes,
But if you didn't mind, sir, on the whole,
I'd rather swap it for another role.
All right, Lord, since I have to play
The beggar, there's one more thing to say.
Why, Lord, did it have to be me?
For the others this play's a comedy
But for me it's a bloody tragedy.
When you handed me my scroll
Didn't you also give me a soul
Equal to his who plays the King
And equal emotions? So that's the thing
Makes us so different? Not our blood.
If you'd moulded us out of different kinds of mud
So I had a more stolid temperament,
Less alive than his, I'd know what you meant.
Lord, you must have something else in mind,
And forgive me, but it does seem unkind
That the King takes a far better role
But he doesn't have a better soul.

DIRECTOR:
If you play the beggar with all your heart
It will please me as much as the King's part.
And when the play is over there will be
Between the two of you, equality.
Play your part well and I promise you this—
Your reward shall be equal to his.
You'll go howling hungry and covered with sores—
But the King's part is no better than yours.
For, under the Law which I have laid,
You are judged by how well your part is played
And what you have earned will then be paid.
After the play, your Director Lord
Will grant all the actors their reward
And the best of the actors shall see my face
And dine with me at my table of Grace.
And at that banquet there shall be
Among you a golden equality.

* * *

WORLD:
Show me your script.

PEASANT:
                    I'd rather not.

WORLD:
You have the look and smell of the land.
Are you to work as a farmhand?

PEASANT:
That's how he cast me. I couldn't say no
But I'd like to say—

WORLD:
                    —You'll be needing this hoe.
(WORLD gives PEASANT a hoe.)

PEASANT:
This is an heirloom left me by Adam
Whose life was ruined by his madam,
For she wheedled him—suck it and see—
And he bit a bit off the fruit from the tree.
Bad acting that, by our begetter.
Still, I don't suppose I'll do any better.
(Exit PEASANT.)

BEGGAR:
I've watched you handing out happiness
But now the game has come round to me.
I don't ask for an embroidered dress
But the rags and patches of misery.

WORLD:
What is your part?

BEGGAR:
                    My part is pain—
Loneliness, sickness, filth, disdain,
Having to beg, never able to give,
Pestering people for the right to live,
Hated by summer, by winter cursed,
Torn by the hounds of hunger and thirst—
All these I shall enact wholeheartedly
For they're essential to true poverty.

WORLD:
I will give you nothing at all.

BEGGAR:
                        No more?
WORLD:
That's all the world ever gives the poor.

In fact I'm afraid I must take this dress
For the poor must suffer from nakedness.
(The WORLD takes dress off the BEGGAR.)

BEGGAR:
So some receive robes and precious stones
While others are stripped down to the bare bones?

WORLD:
Some sing hooray, some sigh alas,
These characters, each from a different class.

* * *

WORLD:
Remind me, please. Could you just say
Which part you acted in the play?

KING:
Has the world so quickly forgotten the King?

WORLD:
The world, my friend, forgets everything.

KING:
I was the diamond, the brilliant one,
Master of every land under the sun.
My crown and robes were of living light,
But now I lie in the arms of night.
I commended, I judged, I achieved great renown,
I explored, I improved, I put enemies down,
I had prudent affairs, I possessed, I enjoyed,
I inherited wealth and I also employed
Thousands of courtiers, servants and cooks
And I wrote three ingenious history books.
You should have seen me when I sat alone
In my golden crown on my golden throne.

WORLD:
Well, take off your crown, take it off, let it be.
Take off your robes and your memory.
(WORLD takes robes and crown from KING.)
Nakedly exit from life's farce.
Your throne shall be filled by another's arse.

Translated from the Spanish by Adrian Mitchell

PIERRE CORNEILLE (1606–1684) was a French playwright and poet. He was born in Rouen in Normandy. He moved to Paris, married and began to write prolifically. In addition to his many secular plays, he also wrote religious dramas.

POLYEUCT

[Polyeuct is a Roman officer in Armenia who has converted to Christianity despite opposition from his wife Pauline and his family, especially his father-in-law Felix. After his death, Polyeuct will be declared a saint.]

From Act 4

POLYEUCT:
Fountain of joys whence untold sorrows spring,
Deceitful pleasures, why not let me be?
Worldly attachments, shameful lusts that cling—
I have abandoned you . . . Abandon me!
Begone, delights—vain honours we amass!
　　All happiness we know
　　Is fragile here below—
　　In no time, it will pass;
　　It twinkles bright as glass
　　But can't survive a blow.

Do not imagine that I still aspire;
In vain, you seek to weave your futile spell!
In vain reveal how, in this vast empire,
God's august enemies in splendour dwell.
Full many a just reverse can God display,

Confounding rich and great—
Suspended swords that wait
The guilty to dismay,
Which none can hope to stay,
For none foresees his fate.

Bloodthirsty tiger, heartless emperor!
Too long God's left his people to your mercies!
Thrice-happy prince, behold what lies in store:
Goths shall avenge Christians alike and Parsees!
It won't be long before you are bereft!
    Your end nought can forestall:
    The thunderbolt to fall!
    The cloud's already cleft;
    For penance, no time left—
    The shaft's beyond recall!

Let Felix sacrifice me to your maw—
Dazzled by my more powerful rival's gleam—
Barter my life for brand-new son-in-law
And, though a slave, to rule this outpost seem:
I'll not object; rather, for death I pine!
    Earth holds no further lure
    My Christian heart now pure,
    Is filled with love divine;
    The wife I thought so fine,
    Salvation made unsure!

O sweets of heaven, which alone are blest,
You rule a heart now ready to receive;
What soul, once by your sacred charms possessed,
Of passion so exciting could conceive?
    You promise much, but even more bestow.
    Your gifts are permanent;
    This happy death I'm sent
    Serves but that I should know
    Whence all those blessings flow,
    Eternally to content!

O fire divine no power on earth can quench,
Now I can face Pauline and never blench;
See her—my heart enflamed by holy zeal—
And charms that once enslaved me, I'll not feel.
My eyes now lit by clear celestial light,
No longer shall find hers exceeding bright.
(Enter PAULINE.)
You asked to see me. What was it you sought—
To thwart my will or offer me support?
This generous gesture, fruit of love complete,
Is meant to help—or hasten my defeat?
You've come to bring me love, or only hate—
As foe, or partner in the married state?

PAULINE:
You *have* no enemies; all love you dearly:
It's you who hate yourself, I speak sincerely—
You, who alone fulfil the dream I dreamt,
Forgo this death-wish, make yourself exempt!
Whatever the gravity of your offence,
Forgive yourself and prove your innocence.
Recall the noble blood that you inherit,
Your valiant feats, rare qualities of merit;
By Prince and people cherished, without flaw:
You are the Province Governor's son-in-law.
Nor do I underrate my husband's title—
A joy to me; for you, it seems, less vital.
With all your exploits, pride in your descent,
And power, the future's hope you represent;
To executioner's blade, pray don't consign
The promise of a destiny so fine!

POLYEUCT:
I've thought of all; my qualities I know—
The hopes brave men on my success bestow.
But what they strive towards are transient gains
Which cares beset and every danger strains;
These are fate's toys which none from death can save:

218

No sooner on the throne, than in the grave.
So great the envy stirred by such distinction,
Few of your Caesars long escape extinction.
The fame I seek's a nobler endeavour.
Their grandeur fades, but mine shall last forever:
A bliss assured, immeasurably great—
Beyond the reach of envy or of fate.
Is this poor life of mine too much to pay?
It can so suddenly be snatched away,
Grants but an instant's joy, so swiftly past,
With no assurance that it's not my last.

PAULINE:
I see you're still obsessed with Christian fancies,
You've been bewitched by all their necromancies!
For bliss so great, blood's not too high a price,
But is that blood your own to sacrifice?
Life is but yours to hold in trust, you know;
From the very moment you are born you owe
Your life to Prince, to public and to State.

POLYEUCT:
I'd die for them in war and bless my fate,
Knowing what joy such death confers—what fame!
The Emperor's forbears, don't you still acclaim—
That name, after six hundred years still precious,
Which placed the Empire in the hands of Decius?
Life I may owe to people, prince and throne—
But how much more to God who made the loan!
If death for Prince be termed a noble fate,
Then death for God's incalculably more great!

PAULINE:
What god?

POLYEUCT:
                Hush! He can hear your every word!
He's not one of your deities absurd—

Impotent, deaf, unfeeling and defaced—
Of marble, wood or gold, to suit man's taste:
He is the Christian God—mine—yours no less:
And none but Him should earth and heaven bless!

* * *

[*Severus is a Roman soldier who attempts to save Polyeuct. Here he is confiding in his servant Fabian. Decius is the current Roman Emperor.*]

SEVERUS:
That warning might impress some simple souls . . .
My life and fortune, Decius controls,
But I'm still Severus! With all his might
My duty he can't change or glory blight.
I am in honour bound and I'll comply;
Let destiny favour me, or hope deny—
For fate is fickle in the last event:
Provided I die well, I'll die content!
And I'll go further, for your private ear:
Christians are not at all what they appear.
He hates them for no reason I can see—
On this point, Decius and I part company.
Being curious, I've come to know them well:
It's claimed that they are wizards ruled by hell;
We punish them with death for their devotion
To mysteries of which we have no notion.
Yet the Good Goddess and Eleusis
Have secret rituals in Rome and Greece:
We tolerate every kind of sect and god—
Apart from Christian. That strikes me as odd.
All Egypt's monsters Roman temples fill;
Our forbears made a god of man at will;
Inheriting their errors in our veins,
Heaven we've peopled with our suzerains.
But, frankly, some of those so highly placed
Would seem to me in questionable taste.

The Christian God in whom all power resides,
Is One alone; His will all else decides.
Whereas, if I may speak in confidence,
Relations between *our* gods are often tense;
And, were their wrath to blast me, in my view,
We've far too many of them to be true.
Moreover, Christians lead much purer lives:
Among them, vice is hateful; virtue thrives;
They even pray for us who persecute them.
However much we torture, execute them—
Since when have Christians mutinied or rebelled?
As soldiers loyal to Rome, why, they've excelled;
Our punishments they endure, however dire—
And, brave as lions, lamb-like they expire.
I pity them too much to scorn her plea:
Let us find Felix; Polyeuct set free!
Only thereby can I, in worthy fashion,
Satisfy Pauline, honour and compassion.

Translated from the French by Noel Clark

PAUL GERHARDT (1607–1676) was a German Lutheran theologian, minister and hymn writer. He was born in the small town of Gräfenhainichen into a middle-class family and studied theology at the University of Wittenberg. He mostly worked as a pastor in and around Berlin. He was married, with one surviving child.

AWAKE, MY HEART, WITH GLADNESS

Awake, my heart, with gladness,
See what today is done;
Now, after gloom and sadness,
Comes forth the glorious sun.
My Savior there was laid
Where our bed must be made
When to the realms of light
Our spirit wings its flight.

The foe in triumph shouted
When Christ lay in the tomb;
But lo, he now is routed,
His boast is turned to gloom.
For Christ again is free;
In glorious victory
He who is strong to save
Has triumphed o'er the grave.

This is a sight that gladdens—
What peace it doth impart!
Now nothing ever saddens
The joy within my heart.
No gloom shall ever shake,
No foe shall ever take
The hope which God's own Son
In love for me hath won.

Now hell, its prince, the devil,
Of all their pow'r are shorn;
Now I am safe from evil,
And sin I laugh to scorn.
Grim death with all his might
Cannot my soul affright;
It is a pow'rless form,
Howe'er it rave and storm.

The world against me rages,
Its fury I disdain;
Though bitter war it wages,
Its work is all in vain.
My heart from care is free,
No trouble troubles me.
Misfortune now is play,
And night is bright as day.

Now I will cling forever
To Christ, my Savior true;
My Lord will leave me never,
Whate'er He passes through.
He rends death's iron chain;
He breaks through sin and pain;
He shatters hell's dark thrall;
I follow Him through all.

He brings me to the portal
That leads to bliss untold,
Whereon this rhyme immortal
Is found in script of gold:
"Who there My cross has shared
Finds here a crown prepared;
Who there with Me has died
Shall here be glorified."

Translated from the German by John Kelly

O Lord, How Shall I Meet You

O Lord, how shall I meet you,
How welcome you aright?
Your people long to greet you,
My hope, my heart's delight!
O kindle, Lord Most Holy,
Your lamp within my breast
To do in spirit lowly
All that may please you best.

Love caused your incarnation,
Love brought you down to me;
Your thirst for my salvation
Procured my liberty.
O love beyond all telling,
That led you to embrace,
In love all love excelling,
Our lost and fallen race!

Rejoice, then, you sad-hearted,
Who sit in deepest gloom,
Who mourn o'er joys departed
And tremble at your doom.
Despair not, he is near you,
Yea, standing at the door,
Who best can help and cheer you
And bids you weep no more.

Sin's debt, that fearful burden,
Let not your souls distress;
Your guilt the Lord will pardon
And cover by his grace.
He comes, for men procuring
The peace of sin forgiv'n,
For all God's sons securing
Their heritage in heav'n.

You come, O Lord, with gladness,
In mercy and goodwill,
To bring an end to sadness
And bid our fears be still.
In patient expectation
We live for that great day
When a renewed creation
Your glory shall display.

Translated from the German by Catherine Winkworth

FRIDRICH BRIDEL (1619–1680) was a Czech Catholic priest and poet. He was born in the town of Vysoké Mýto and entered the Jesuit order in Prague at 18. He taught theology at Charles University and ran the Jesuit press in Prague. He later devoted himself to missionary activity in Bohemia, where he died of plague.

FROM *WHAT IS GOD? MAN?*

Three-cornered and three-sided, you
are both triangular and round;
A spherical abyss far too
immeasurably deep to sound;
you are justice, but with no
plumb line, cord, or bounden duty.
Ageless, unadorned you go,
clad in wholly perfect beauty.

Flawless beauty that you are,
and happy beyond every joy,
greater than all love by far,
your purity without alloy
is too clean for time to touch you,
age deface you, force defy,
treasure own you, or death clutch you:
eternal, you can never die.

You are what perfect truth there is.
Since only perfect things can be,
all things, and man, as things are his,
wants to be yours eternally.
You are earth, but still unploughed;
you are the ocean, but still dry,
where no storm blows wild and loud.
You are god, most great, most high.

The unexplained is your disguise:
the unkindled, smokeless flame;
wind—the air on which you rise;
the sea without its seashore frame;
a valley waiting for its hill;
the sun without its morning gleam
or sunset glow; and strangely still,
that flowless interrupted stream.

You are roses with no thorn;
sourceless well; beginning; ending;
all as it was when newly born;
flawless love that needs no mending;
wine unfermented; grapes unpressed;
book without words that makes no sound;
sound not yet voice, still unaddressed;
you everywhere, as yet unfound.

Grove are you, but with no shade;
pure gold mined without the tailing;
beauty no cosmetic made;
glorious throne behind its veiling;
heaven by the light of day;
sea without the waves grown wild;
health that keeps disease away;
laughter, but serene and mild.

You're a garden with no hedge;
speech without tongue; and without rind
you are fruit; you are the edge
of the abyss no sight can find,
where I drown, dark in that light,
under the homeland that I love:
wholly immersed, and out of sight,
far from all that lives above.

Now I ask, What is my god?
Everything here confuses me!
I wander; everything seems odd.
I'm baffled by the deity.
I can't make sense of god: however
I prod my mind to comprehend,
however hard I try, I never
pursue god's nature to the end.

What kind of night awaits me now,
I'm wondering, untangling such
imponderable thoughts as how
great god is? And more—so much!
I'm purified enough to think
such thoughts, to laugh like this, and be
ready to drown in them, and sink
while pondering divinity!

Translated from the Czech by Rhina P. Espaillat with Henry R. Cooper, Jr.

ANGELUS SILESIUS (c. 1624–1677), born JOHANN SCHEFFLER, was a German Catholic priest, physician, mystic and poet. He was born in Breslau in present-day Poland and studied medicine and science at the Universities of Strasbourg and Leiden. He was raised as a Lutheran, but, after being persecuted by Protestant authorities for his increasing mysticism, he converted to Catholicism and was ordained a priest.

FROM *THE CHERUBINIC PILGRIM*

1.66. *My Heart is God's Stove*

If God is like a fire, my heart the stove must be,
In which his heat consumes the wood of vanity.

1.80. *Each in his own element*

The bird is in the air, the stone rests on the land,
The fish lives in the water, my spirit in God's hand.

1.103. *Spiritual alchemy*

I am the metal heated in the Spirit's stove and fire,
And what transforms me is the tincture, the Messiah.

1.104. *On the same*

No sooner in God's fire have I been melted down
Than with his seal he stamps my essence as his own.

1.145. *You are what you will*

Heaven lies within you, and Hell's pain is also there:
What you have willed and chosen is with you everywhere.

1.153. *You must become a child*

You must become a child or you will never go
Where all God's children are: the door is much too low.

2.25. *The unrest comes from you*

It's not from God or creatures that your disquiet springs:
You make your own unrest (O fool!) by your concern with things.

2.53. *Only you fall short*

If you could make your heart a manger for his birth
God would become once more a child upon this earth.

2.69. *The spiritual voyage*

The world's my sea, God's Spirit is my captain in command,
My body is the ship in which my soul comes home to land.

2.153. *Eternity*

What is eternity? It is not this nor that;
Not now, not then, not nothing; it is I know not what.

3.98. *Not to feign is not to sin*

What is it, not to sin? Ah sinner, ask no more;
The speechless flowers will tell you, if you step out of doors.

3.102. *The way to the Creator*

O wretched mortal man, stay not so long in thrall
To the base gaudy loves and colors of this world;
The beauty of creation is but a bridge at best,
Leading to the creator in whom all beauties rest.

3.112. *The heart is immense*

The heart that time and space can fully gratify
Has still not understood its own immensity.

3.116. *Elements of the spiritual sacrifice*

The altar is my heart, the priest is my own soul;
The victim is my will, and love the burning coal.

4.66. *On Mary Magdalen*

Ah, what can she be thinking of, poor Mary Magdalen,
To fall confessing at Christ's feet before the eyes of men?
Ask not, but look upon her eyes, and marvel how they shine:
Is it not clear that she has drunk too deeply of love's wine?

4.119. *The barrel must be clean*

Wash out the barrel of your heart: should any yeast remain,
God will no longer come to you and fill it with his wine.

4.194. *What God most loves to do*

Of all the works that God most dearly loves to do
The best is that he brings his Son to birth in you.

5.278. *The spiritual crabwalk*

Lower yourself, my friend, to gain the highest place;
As soon as you stop running, you can begin the race.

6.104. *All earthly things must go*

Unless you can throw overboard what you love best on earth,
Your ship will not in Heaven's port find its eternal berth.

6.262. *The world is a grain of sand*

How does the world prevent us from seeing God on high?
It is a grain of sand that irritates the eye.

6.263. *Conclusion*

Enough, my friend. Would you read more? Go hence,
And make yourself the writing and the sense.

Translated from the German by Anthony Mortimer

Wu Li (1632–1718) was a Chinese priest, poet, painter and calligrapher. He was born in Changzhou and became one of China's greatest painters. He converted to Catholicism in mid-life, entered the Jesuit order and spent seven years training in Macau. He then spent his final years as a priest in rural China.

SINGING OF THE SOURCE AND COURSE OF HOLY CHURCH

1

Within the twelvefold walled enclosure,
    at the highest spot
is the palace of the Lord
    with springs and autumns of its own.
The misty fragrance is breath of flowers
    where roses bloom;
the glittering brilliance is glow of pearls
    where gemmed crowns reverently bow.
There in Heaven should we seek
    true blessings and true joy;
in the human realm we must cut off
    false strivings and false plans.
Look there where girls, so many of them,
    their hair in tufts,
day after day follow behind
    the Holy Mother in their play.

2

Before the firmament was ever formed,
    or any foundation laid,
high there hovered the Judge of the World,
    prepared for the last days!
This single Man from His five wounds
    poured every drop of blood;
    a myriad nations gave their hearts
    to the wonder of the Cross!
The heavenly gates now have a ladder
    leading to their peace;
demonic spirits lack any art
    to insinuate deception.
Take up the burden, joyfully
    fall in behind Jesus,
look up with reverence towards the top of that mountain,
    follow His every step.

3

Primal chaos of myriad ages—
    orifices were bored, breath blown into them.
The single globule of earth
    rolled among heavenly powers and bodies.
Flowers flourished, cicadas droned,
    in perfect correspondence;
snow darkened sky, wind fiercely blew,
    each quite unawares.
In the Old Testament
    there was no essence of life;
the spiritual source had in store
    another wondrous proposal.
These words of advice and admonishment
    retain, Sir, in your ear:
imprint them against the time when you
    will have no words to say.

4

One day, when a baby boy came down to earth,
He had not the slightest sin;
    now such a thing is rare!
From Heaven He descended,
    how blessed, oh how blessed!
By a woman he was born,
    how wondrous, oh how wondrous!
All the saints sighed in admiration
    stretched forward for a look;
the myriad regions leapt and danced,
    joy in all expressions.
The one once promised to be with us has come to comfort
    us: remember

Translator's note: I am unable to determine the meaning of the last line.

5

I used to chant that poem of Chou
    about "ascending and descending":
it was like clouds or fogs dispersing,
    so I could see the azure sky.
I never suspected a world of brilliance
    double that of sun and moon
would start with the year *keng-shen*
    of the *Yuan-shou* reign.
Learning then had new knowledge
    with blessings pure imbued;
the Way attained far-reaching care,
    the holy work complete.
I wish to follow cloud-pendants of jade
    to hear exalted singing;
how could the pearl of the black dragon alone
    serve to illuminate that poem?

Translator's note: The translation of the last line is tentative; I am uncertain of the relevant allusion.

6

By nature I have always felt quite close to the Way;
when done with chanting my new poems,
    I always concentrate my spirit.
Prior to death, who believes
    in the joy of the land of Heaven?
After the end, then comes amazement
    at the truth of the fires of hell!
The achievements and fame of this ephemeral world:
    footprints of geese on snow;
this body, this shell in a lifetime of toil:
    dust beneath horses' hoofs.
    And what is more, the flowing of time
    presses man so fast:
let us plan to ask carefully about the ford
    that leads to the true source.

7

Teeth and hair infused with spirit—
 this we call a man;
the great Father of all heaven and earth
 is the truth in human nature.
At least we know the "fern" supreme;
 the heavenly task is clear.
This indeed is the "orchid terrace"
 the child is meant to seek out.
For past events we deeply grieve,
 a thousand gallons of tears!
Future happiness is surely foretold,
 spring in every season!
Not merely because of favoring a teaching
 have we started a new teaching:
let us strive for faith that we shall live forever
 in blessings and in peace.

Translator's note: The translation of lines 3 and 4 is tentative and based on the assumption that Wu Li intends allusions to poem 14 in the *Shih ching* and to the lost *Shih ching* poem, *Nan-kai*. The former poem associates the plucking of ferns with longing for a lord whom the speaker is missing (or has not yet met). Karlgren translates the key lines as follows: "I ascend that southern mountain, I gather the *wei* plant; when I have not yet seen the lord, my heart is pained, but when I have seen him, when I have met him, my heart is at ease." See Bernhard Karlgren, *The Book of Odes* (Stockholm: Museum of Far Eastern Antiquities, 1950), p. 9. The preface to the lost *Nan-kai* poem links it with *hsiao* (filial piety) and *yu* (friendship). The third-century scholar Shu Hsi wrote a poem to take the place of this lost ode, which includes the lines *hsün pi nan kai, / yen ts'ai ch'i lan* ("I seek that southern terrace, / indeed to pluck the orchid there"). See Morohashi Tetsuji, *Daikanwa jiten* (Tokyo: 1955-1959), 2:1648-1649. It seems possible that Wu Li's use of these allusions is intended to suggest that Christ is the true Lord and his father the true Father and friend, but this interpretation must remain tentative.

8

In the very highest place, deep within a mansion
dwells a family perfectly united, loving and devoted.
Beyond past, beyond present, the three Persons are one;
penetrating heaven, penetrating earth,
    the one family is three!
Those who are known as "daily improving"
    to praise the Spirit are worthy;
The world possesses a wondrous flower
    fit to protect the holy.
On painted walls, year after year,
    we contemplate their images:
pure incense rises in orderly spirals
    to where their noses inhale.

9

In glory they are crowned in jade,
    and clothed in robes of gold;
Their merit earned in bloody battle,
    childlike their hearts.
A valley of ten thousand colors,
    fragrances and flowers;
a forest from a single root,
    a single trunk and vine.
To soul's repletion, intoxicated
    they drink from the cup of Jesus;
with dancing limbs, they stretch forward to listen
    to the harp of David.
"Holy, Holy, Holy," their voices ceaselessly cry:
beneath the throne of the Lamb
    echoes the sound of their song.

10

Utterly transcendent, His wondrous essence
    was never limited to place;
to bring life to the teeming people
    He showed Himself, then hid.
Effortlessly, a single standard—
    a new cake baked for us;
as before, the six directions have one supreme Lord.
In the human realm, now we have
    a whole burnt offering;
in Heaven for eternity is preserved our daily bread.
I have incurred so many transgressions,
    yet am allowed to draw near:
with body and soul fully sated,
    tears moisten my robe.

11

"The Supreme Ultimate contains three"—
    muddled words indeed!
In fact, they start with primal energy
    to speak of original chaos.
From books of the past, we learned of old
    of sincerity, wisdom, and goodness;
the mysterious meaning now we understand
    of Father, Son, and Holy Spirit.
The Persons distinct: close at hand, consider
    the flame within the mirror;
The Essence is whole: far off, please note
    the wheel that graces the sky.
The Holy Name has been revealed,
    His authority conferred;
throughout the world in this human realm,
    the sound of the teaching supreme!

12

The flower of the twelvefold heavens
    ornaments the colored clouds,
crown jewel for a new knit robe
    worthy of the Holy Mother.
The hues have been bestowed
    from the midst of light with no beginning;
the fragrance has been absorbed
    from the love of the primordial womb.
Miraculous, that a single Virgin
    should give blossom to this precious bloom;
glorious that ten thousand saints
    should throng towards the splendid audience!
What day will we receive the blessing
    of entering His court,
His beauteous visage ourselves to see,
    each face suffused with joy?

Translator's note: The translation of line 6 is tentative.

Translated from the Chinese by Jonathan Chaves

CATHARINA REGINA VON GREIFFENBERG (1633–1694) was an Austrian Lutheran noblewoman and poet. She was born in the village of Viehdorf, west of Vienna, and educated there by her uncle and guardian, whom she would eventually marry under duress. As Catholic Austria became more restrictive, she eventually settled in Nuremburg.

ON THE UNQUENCHABLE NOBLE ART OF POETRY

Let no one dare deny me heaven's gentle gifts:
    the invisible ray, resounding mystery,
    that rare, angelic artistry. This alone,
    in time and after time, when all is done, remains.
Wit, wonder and delight, set free from darkness,
    keep pace with eternity:
    the sun at midnight streaming rays of light
    that, unforbidden, all, in every circumstance, may savour.
This gift alone is freely given me, who otherwise must be
    a slave to overwhelming might of pure misfortune.
    Here, in this freedom, will my spirit prove
all I endeavour serves this end alone:
    O God, your honour I will raise above all else.
    Grant me this freedom, and eternally I'll praise you.

On Christ's Miracle Birth

What! Has the All moved into nothingness?
    The Inexpressible, expressing everything,
    has made of weakness its omnipotent dwelling
    and lifts a footstool up to be the Honour-Throne?
The Incomprehensible desires to rest on human hands.
    He who stirs earth and heaven with thunder-roar—
    what's more! turns sea to stone with his swift breath—
    intends to dwell inside that modest glass: the virgin's body.
The One whose word and wisdom-power has birthed all being
    deigns to be given birth out of the dust of time.
    God becomes man: now man can be unlost.
His suffering-abyss raises you to heavenly honour.
    Abandon pomp and pride! The Exalted One appoints
    humility as essence of all greatness. Follow Him.

On the Glorious Wonder of God's Reign

Oh you whose wisdom dews the stars, the source
    of destiny—and yet without their work
    your art alone brings everything to pass, displays your strength
    from which heaven's powers, in highest meekness, flee!
Your royal staff streams light of righteousness and goodness.
    Rapt in wonder, I mark your tender care
    for your creation's crown as for the slightest speck.
    No fiery angel-mind attains your loving-kindness.
You spin a happiness-web of a thousand threads:
    in all the starry spheres, in all earth-places,
    all effort must be offered to the work that you begin.
Your all-providing power prepares the way.
    You pull the cord to which all hearts are clinging
    and bring the mind's design, through action, into being.

THE MIRROR OF GOD'S PROVIDENCE

The ark was floating, Lord God, in your mind
    while the heavens were troubled and floodwaters rose.
    Before the old world drowned, the wide world's hero
    stood live, at your decree, upon the stage.
The fire had cooled before those three were in it
    and David, too, was crowned while still in misery,
    the woman plucked to safety before the dragon snatched her.
    It is God's way: to spin a cord before a mortal goes astray.
The serpent was unfanged before Paul touched it;
    the gospel-light shone bright in God's foreknowledge
    before one spark of it was felt in human souls.
Before misfortune strikes, the Highest is alert to help;
    so: follow him. However strange or curious his leading,
    his hand tears free from hell and misery.

ON THE HOLY SPIRIT'S WONDROUS CONSOLATION

Refreshment from on high, heart-quickening breath!
    You heavenly balm! In suffering, Joy-Spirit
    that comforts while defying death and trouble,
    and calls forth in us joy more plenteous than sorrow.
O let my life behold your heart-illumination!
    Let misery be mocked while you are ever praised,
    and I by you sustained with health and strength.
    Waft over troubled waters, as when the world began.
You good God-Spirit, pain-conqueror, overthrow
    the soul-deceiver; let not his heart-tormenting fire
    consume faith's oil in my lamp;
let not his torturous grappling-hooks ensnare me.
    Bedew my rose, O sweet soul's dew, so she
    may rise up through your cooling strength.

The Wonder-Work of Incarnation

The Cup of Life is given mother-milk to drink.
    The Conqueror of the whole wide world
    lies in a narrow manger.
    The Lord of Heaven offers himself to Earth;
the Highest Good descends to lowest misery.
    See the Prime Mover gently cradle-rocked
    from whom heaven itself receives
    order and obligation for its course.
Shepherds! Leave the heavens!
    Go now to the stable.
    Have you ever heard
of such amazing Wonder-Work?
    Weakness has borne strength
    and a star, the sun.

On the Death of My Chosen Jesus

O worship-worthy miracle! Will Life now die?
    The Fountain of vitality run dry? Eternal Light extinguish?
    Will the Source of sap and strength be sapped of strength?
    Will the Arch-Force that sustains all destroy itself?
We inherit from his death forever-life.
    The uttermost utterance of the godhead-power story
    creates destruction deep in hell's domain.
    The Immortal gains immortality in death—
death and life, he swallows both.
    From Jesus' end ensues my eternal bliss.
    Through weakness, Strength has overcome
the strongest enemy of man. He, free from death,
    died willingly; now what is mortal lives eternally.
    Entombed, he freed the spirits from the grave.

Translated from the German by Sarah Klassen, Joanne Epp and Sally Ito

THOMAS KINGO (1634–1703) was a Danish Lutheran bishop, poet and hymn writer. He was born at Slangerup, near Copenhagen, into a weaver's family, and studied at the University of Copenhagen. He served as minister in Slangerup and later as Bishop of Funen. He was married three times and compiled a new official Danish hymn book, which included many of his own compositions.

JESUS' SWEAT IN THE GARDEN

Over Kedron Jesus treadeth
To His passion for us all;
Every human eye be weeping,
Tears of bitter grief let fall!
Round His spirit flock the foes,
Place their shafts and bend their bows,
Aiming at the Saviour solely,
While the world forsakes Him wholly.

David once, with heart afflicted,
Crossed the Kedron's narrow strand,
Clouds of gloom and grief about him
When an exile from his land.
But, O Jesus, blacker now
Bends the cloud above Thy brow,
Hasting to death's dreary portals
For the shame and sin of mortals.

Wilt Thou in Thy pain and ruing
To the Mount of Olives go?
Yet there is no tree for viewing
Where the fruits of peace may grow;
War and battle, bitter pain,
Death and mockery and shame
Every bud shoots forth with sorrow
Jesus now no peace can borrow.

Enter now the restful garden
As a peaceful quiet space,
Sorrow soon begins to darken,
Follow Thee in every place!
Come now, Adam, come and see
Enter blest Gethsemane!
See the Lord of heaven shaking
Hellish anguish for us taking.

All of Jesus' limbs are quaking
As sins' burden hard doth press
See the God-Man ever shaking
Death doth bring to life distress
Jesus' lifeblood forth doth pour
And His heart aches more and more
Shooting forth with blood-streams narrow
From ten thousand poisoned arrows.

See how, anguish-struck, He falleth
Prostrate, and with struggling breath,
Three times on His God He calleth,
Praying that the bitter death
And the cup of doom may go,
Still He cries, in all His woe:
"Not My will, but Thine, O Father!"
And the angels round Him gather.

See how, in that hour of darkness,
Battling with the evil power,
Agonies untold assail Him,
On His soul the arrows shower;
All the garden flowers are wet
With the drops of bloody sweat,
From His anguished frame distilling—
World's redemption thus fulfilling!

O ye heavéns, will ye give Him
Strength of heart, and that right soon?
To the end He hard has striven
Jesus dies! He dies so soon!
Holy angels, come and see
Strengthen Him for death to see!
How His cheeks are filled with pallor,
As He meets His death with valor.

See the blood so sadly dripping
With each drop of sweat so cold;
Death in every vein is seeping
And His face is dark as coal;
And the grass where Jesus prays
Now a bloody carpet stays
From His precious veins now offering,
See what pains He now is suffering!

Daily I am gladly yearning
E'er to go to Kedron's stream
And from earthly pleasure turning
In a penitential theme!
Daily in Gethsemane
With my spirit I shall see
Jesus' bleeding and His sighing
For my soul is all His dying.

Now, away with earthly pleasure!
Let me see my Jesus dear!
In Gethsemane, my Treasure,
I will gather me a tear
From His bloody sweat of pain
Which my righteousness did gain
Earth now gives me only sadness
Till I enter heaven's gladness.

But, O flowers, so sadly watered
By this pure and precious dew,
In some blessed hour your blossoms
'Neath the olive-shadows grew!
Eden's garden did not bear
Aught that can with you compare,
For the blood, thus freely given,
Makes my soul the heir of heaven.

When as flowers themselves I wither,
When I droop and fade like grass,
When the life-streams through my pulses
Dull and ever duller pass,
When at last they cease to roll,
Then, to cheer my sinking soul,
Grace of Jesus, be Thou given—
Source of triumph! pledge of heaven!

And now when my heart is breaking,
And my eye no longer sees,
When my tongue no sound is making,
Let my soul a droplet seize
Of Thy precious sweat and blood;
Wash my heart in that dear flood.
In the hour when I am dying,
On Thy Passion I'm relying.

Translated from the Danish by J.A. Jeffrey and Mark DeGarmeaux

Jean Racine (1639–1699) was a French playwright. He was born in Picardy in northern France and raised by his Jansenist grandmother at the Port-Royal Abbey in Paris. As a writer, he was known for his tragedies on Classical themes. After his marriage, he became highly devout and retired from the theatre, only to return for two final religious plays, *Esther* and *Athalia*.

ATHALIA

From Act 4, Scene 3

AZARIAH:
We pledge our word—our brethren's *and* our own—
To establish Joash on his father's throne
And not lay down these weapons you bestow
Till we've avenged him on his every foe.
If some transgressor fails to keep his word,
Let Your unbridled vengeance strike him, Lord:
That, with his sons, denied Your blessed lot,
He rank amongst the dead whom You know not.

JEHOIADA:
And to the Lord's eternal Law do you,
My king, swear that you always will be true?

JOASH:
His righteous Law how could I not obey?

JEHOIADA:
My son—I'll call you that still, if I may—
Suffer this tenderness; forgive these tears
Which flow for your sake from my too just fears.
Brought up far from the throne, you're unaware
Of the envenomed charms that wait you there:

Absolute power can intoxicate,
And fawning, flattering voices fascinate;
Our sacred laws—so they'll be counseling—
Rule the vile people, but *obey* the king;
From all constraints, they'll say, kings should be free;
Their *will* should be their sole authority:
All else must bow before their majesty;
Only to weep, to work, are most men fit,
And to an iron scepter would submit;
If they are not oppressed, *they* will oppress.
And thus, from snare to snare, abyss to abyss,
Corrupting your pure heart, your pristine youth,
They'll make you, in the end, despise the truth,
Painting fair virtue as a frightful thing.
Alas! they led astray our wisest king.
Swear on this book, and let all hear your swear.
That God will always be your foremost care;
That, scourging wickedness, shielding the just,
When judging of the poor, in God you'll trust,
Recalling that, beneath your linen dress,
You once, like them, were poor and fatherless.

JOASH:
I swear to do as the Law bids me do.
Chastise me, Lord, if I abandon You.

JEHOIADA:
Come, holy unction now must consecrate you.
— Stand forth now, Josabeth: we all await you.

Translated from the French by Geoffrey Alan Argent

Sor Juana Inés de la Cruz (1648–1695) was a Mexican nun, writer, philosopher, composer and poet. She was the illegitimate daughter of a Spanish captain and a wealthy young Mexican woman. She was a child prodigy and became well-known at the court of the viceroy for her learning. She became a nun in order to devote herself to art and philosophy. Near the end of her life, she was forced to stop writing because because she was a woman and died of the plague soon after.

From *First Dream*

My understanding desired to follow
the method of this series,
that is, to pass from the lowest degree of
inanimate being (least favored if not
most unprotected of all produced by the
second cause), to the nobler ranking that in
vegetal life is first born, although crude, of
Thetis (the first who at her
fertile maternal breasts with
attractive virtue expressed
the sweet springs of terrestrial humor that
as natural sustenance is the sweetest food),
a ranking adorned by four
diverse, quite contrary acts,
which attracts, then diligently segregates
what it deems unsuitable,
expels the superfluous, and makes the most
useful substances its own;
and (once investigated)
probes a more beautiful form
(adorned with senses and more
than senses apprehensive
imaginative power),
that with reason can give rise to a dispute,

when not an insult to the inanimate
star that gleams and shines most bright
with haughty splendor, for the
lowest creature, the most humble can provoke
envy, possess advantage;
and making of this bodily knowledge the
foundation, however meager, moves on to
the supreme, the marvelous, the tripartite
composite ordered of three harmonious
lines and of all lower forms
a mysterious recapitulation:
a decisive joining of pure nature raised
to the heights, enthroned, and the
least noble, the most contemptible creature:
adorned not only with the five faculties
of sense but ennobled by
the three directing internal ones, the gift,
and not in vain, of a wise, powerful hand,
to be mistress of the rest:
the zenith of His works, the circle that joins
the sphere and earth, ultimate perfection of
creation and ultimate
delight of the Eternal Creator, and
in whom, satisfied, His vast magnificence
came to rest, portentous origination:
no matter how haughtily it reaches for
heaven, dust closes its mouth,
its mysterious image
might be the sacred vision that the Eagle
of the Evangels saw in Patmos, which walked
among the stars and on earth with equal steps,
or the huge statue whose rich high head of the
most precious metal was made,
its base of the most scorned and weakest substance,
shattered at the least motion:
man, I say, in short, the greatest wonder that
human understanding can devise, absolute
compendium that resembles the angels,

the plants, the brutes; whose exalted lowliness
partakes of all of nature.
Why? Perhaps because more fortunate than the
rest, it is elevated
by the grace of a loving union. And oh,
grace, though repeated, never well enough known
as it seems to be ignored
so little valued and so unrequited!

Translated from the Spanish by Edith Grossman

GASPAR AQUINO DE BELÉN (late 1600s–early 1700s) was a Filipino priest and poet. He was born in Rosario, south of Manila, into a wealthy family. He joined the Jesuit Order and ran the Jesuit press in Manila during the early 1700s.

FROM *THE SACRED PASSION OF OUR LORD JESUS CHRIST*

Jesus stood up with this to say:
"My dearest ones, I cannot stay
long past this blessed holy day.
The time has come: I must obey
God's orders, and then go my way."

After the solemn words he said,
he ordered supper: lamb and bread
Saint Peter and Saint John had spread—
and more—before them. Then they fed,
and Jesus spoke of days ahead.

They listened closely, all together
surrounding him, their Lord and Father,
exchanging looks with one another
as in a family, each brother
looks to the others in rough weather.

"Dearest companions, friends I trust,
how I have longed to join you, best
of all Apostles, at this tryst
to celebrate the Paschal feast,
before our time as friends is past!

"Though I have warned you that, for me—
the Second Person of the Three
who form the Holy Trinity—
only great pain and death will be,
as you, my brothers, soon will see.

"This supper is our very last
chance to rejoice and break our fast
together, each both host and guest:
when my last hour on earth has passed,
our former friendship, too, is lost.

"And you should know a trap's been laid
against my life: an ambuscade,
a plan that enemies have made
with one of us, to be well paid
in silver, once I've been betrayed."

Saint Peter, taken by surprise,
searched for the truth in startled eyes.
Now, one by one they agonize:
"Am I the one?" as they surmise
who is the traitor in disguise.

Bewildered by this painful scene,
close to Saint John Saint Peter leans
to ask him if—and by what means—
they might unmask one so unclean
as to betray the Nazarene.

Saint John, whose heart with sorrow burns,
questions the Lord, eager to learn
who is the cause of their concern,
to ease their hearts, and overturn
the plotter with the pain he's earned.

Jesus replies with just a clue:
"Watch me to see what I will do.
If I break bread with one of you,
he is the one, the traitor who
feigns friendship, but is all untrue."

For a hard heart there is no cure.
Like quartz, unyielding; to endure,
not to be moved, but lurk secure
in the dark prison of its pure,
unloving, cold discomfiture.

Dinner continued; Jesus rose
radiant with beauty, and composed;
said nothing of what he proposed,
but filled a basin that he chose,
and wrapped a towel around his clothes.

Peter was first. Down Jesus knelt,
undid the towel like a belt,
and the Apostles then beheld
foot-washing: rite unparalleled
that speaks of love wordlessly felt.

Peter leapt back in shocked distress,
as if to say, "My Lord, what's this?"
And then he said, *Non lalabis
in aeternum mihi pedes!*"
And he refused to acquiesce.

"Heaven and Earth may well indict,"
he said, "and have you in their sight
if I accept what seems a slight
to your divinity! Yes, quite!
This rite, Lord Jesus, is not right!"

Jesus replied, "If you intend
to thwart me, and refuse to bend
your will to God's, then in the end
you'll cease to be the loyal friend
on whom I thought I could depend.

"You will no longer, from now on,
Be my beloved companion,
or share with me the benison
of heaven's grace and peace, withdrawn
wholly from you, forever gone."

When good Saint Peter clearly heard
his dearest friend pronounce those words,
his very soul was deeply stirred,
and he replied, "Teacher and Lord,
command me, for I have concurred!

"You who made everything in sight,
do not deprive me of your light
beloved by day, longed for by night;
exile from you would be a plight
bereaving me of all delight!"

Jesus the just now too replied:
"Do as I do, stand by my side,
guide others as I am your guide,
lead where I lead you, and abide,
old friend in whom I can confide."

Then, when the others saw those two
bound by a compact forged anew
after debate, the retinue
had their feet washed: dissension through,
gladly they chose God's will to do.

After the Lord had washed their feet,
his satisfaction now complete
and his will done, he took his seat
and said, in words tender and sweet,
why he had gathered them to eat.

"Have you, my comrades and most dear,
guessed why I wished to bring you here?
I have a gift—a souvenir—
meant to remind you, year by year,
to love each other, far or near,

"And that our mission is divine,
with heaven's purposes aligned.
On this, the last day we shall dine,
let us recall this, as a sign
that I am yours and you are mine.

"Let not this moment come to naught,
nor what together we have wrought;
come taste my meat—reject it not;
come sip my wine—more bled than bought;
do not forget what I have taught."

Translated from the Tagalog by Rhina P. Espaillat with René B. Javellana

WILLIAM WILLIAMS PANTYCELYN (1717–1791) was a Welsh Methodist
preacher, hymn writer and poet. He was born on a farm near Llandovery in
the south of Wales into a Non-conformist family. He joined the Anglican
Church, but was rejected for priesthood because of his Methodist leanings.
He then lived and worked out of Llandovery as an independent preacher
and church organizer.

THE LOVE OF GOD

Always across the distant hills
I'm looking for you yet;
Come, my beloved, it grows late
And my sun has almost set.

Each and every love I had
Turned unfaithful to me at length;
But a sweet sickness has taken me
Of a love of mightier strength.

A love the worldly don't recognise
For its virtue or its grace,
But it sucks my liking and desire
From every creature's face.

O make me faithful while I live,
And aimed level at thy praise,
Let no object under the sky
Take away my gaze!

But pull my affections totally
From falsities away
To the one object that keeps faith
And shall for ever stay.

Nothing under the blue air now
Would make me want to live
But only that I'll know the joys
That the courts of God can give.

Relish and appetite have died
For the flowers of the world that fall:
Only a vanity without ebb
Is running through it all.

Pilgrim

Pilgrim I am in a desert land,
    Wandering far and late,
In expectation, every hour,
    I near my Father's gate.

In front of me I think I hear
    Sounds of a multitude—
They that have conquered and gone through
    Fire and tempestuous flood.

Come, Holy Spirit, a fire by night,
    A pillar of cloud by day,—
I will not venture half a step
    Unless you lead the way.

This way or that I miss the path
    And fall to either side—
Oh, to that paradise, step by step,
    Go before me, God my guide!

I've longing on me for that land
    Where the unnumbered throng
Anthem the death on Calvary
    Even as their lives are long.

Fair Weather

I see that the black clouds
Now almost disappear,
The north wind that was loud
Begins slowly to veer,
And after high tempest soon shall roll
Fair weather to my fainting soul.

The black night shall not toss
Nor for long the storm rage,
No man to carry the cross
Is dealt too long an age;
Delightful is yon rising dawn
Promising soon a glorious morn.

I look across the hills
Of my Father's house, and see
The sunlight on the ground
Whose grace sets me free:
That in Life's book my name is writ
And no man blots or cancels it.

And though in the desert night
I've wandered many a year
And often had to drink
Of the bitter cup, despair;
The yoke I suffered was my gain
And not for nothing came that pain.

The burden on my back
Pulled heaven down to earth,
It sanctified for me
All woe and grievous dearth:
The wheel turned to my fervent prayer,
The bitterest bile was sweetened there.

The chastenings of heaven,
Lashed by the Father's thong,
Are sweet like honeycombs
With healing blithe and long:
By cross and grief, by tempest driven,
The saints are ripened into heaven.

Translated from the Welsh by Tony Conran

GAVRILA DERZHAVIN (1743 – 1816) was a Russian poet and statesman. He was born into a poor but noble family near the city of Kazan, where he was also educated. He eventually rose to become provincial governor, then personal secretary to Catherine the Great and, finally, Minister of Justice, before retiring to his estate near Novogrod.

GOD

O Thou, in universe so boundless,
alive in planets as they swarm
within eternal flow, yet timeless,
unseen, you reign in triune form!
Thy single Spirit all comprises,
from no abode or cause arises,
keeps paths that Reason never trod,
pervades, incarnate, all that's living,
embracing, keeping and fulfilling,
to Thee we give the name of GOD!

To put the ocean depths to measure,
to sum the sands, the planet's rays,
a lofty mind might want at leisure—
but knows no rule for Thee, nor scales!
Nor can the spirits brought to seeing,
born from Thy light into their being,
trace the enigmas of Thy ways:
our thought, with daring, space traverses,
approaching Thee, in Thee disperses,—
a blink in the Abyss—no trace.

Thou didst call forth great Chaos's presence
from out the timeless, formless deep,
and then didst found Eternal essence,
before the Ages born in Thee:
within Thyself didst Thou engender
Thy selfsame radiance's splendour,
Thou art that Light whence flows light's beam.
Thine ageless Word from the beginning
unfolded all, for aye conceiving,
Thou wast, Thou art and Thou shalt be!

The chain of Being Thou comprisest,
and dost sustain it, give it breath;
End and Beginning Thou combinest,
dost Life bestow in Thee through death.
As sparks disperse, surge upward, flying,
so suns are born from Thee, undying;
as on those cold, clear winter's days
when specks of hoarfrost glisten, shimmer,
gyrate and whirl—from chasms' glimmer
so Stars cast at Thy feet bright rays.

Those billions of lumens flaming
flow through the measureless expanse,
they govern laws, enforce Thy bidding,
they pour forth life in gleaming dance.
Yet all those lampions thus blazing,
those scarlet heaps with crystal glazing,
or rolling mounds of golden waves,
all ethers in their conflagration,
each world aflame in its own station—
to Thee—they are as night to day.

A drop of water in the ocean:
such is Creation in Thy sight.
What sets the Cosmos into motion?
And what—before Thee—what am I?
Should I count worlds, afloat by billions
in heaven's seas on unseen pinions,
and multiply them hundredfold,
then dare compare to Thee their measure,
they'd form a blot for quick erasure:
and so, before Thee, I am Naught.

Before Thee, Naught!—And yet Thy brightness
shines forth through me by Thy good grace;
Thou formest in me Thine own likeness,
as in a drop Sol finds its trace.
But Naught?—Yet Life in me is calling,
uplifts me in an upward soaring
beyond the clouds my course to chart;
in search of Thee my Spirit wanders,
it reasons, contemplates and ponders:
I am—assuredly, Thou art!

Thou art! Thus claim the laws of Nature,
this Truth my heart has erstwhile known,
it gives my mind the strength to venture:
Thou art!—No naught, my Self I own!
Made part of universal order,
and set, meseems, not on its border,
but in Creation's central site,
whence crowned Thou Earth with creatures living,
with light celestial spirits filling,
and linked through me their chain of life.

I bind all worlds Thou hast created,
creation's top and crown am I,
to be Life's centre I am fated,
where mortal borders on Divine.
My body sinks to endless slumber,
and yet my mind commands the thunder,
a king—a slave—a worm—a god!
I am most marvellously fashioned,
yet, whence came I? I cannot fathom:
myself could not this self have wrought.

Thy creature am I, O Creator!
Thy wisdom shaped me, gave me form,
blest Giver, Life's Originator,
O Soul of mine own soul—my Lord!
to Thy Truth was it necessary
for my immortal soul to carry
its life, unscathed, o'er Death's abyss,
my spirit should don mortal cover,
so that I might return, O Father,
through death to Thine immortal bliss.

Ungraspable, beyond all knowledge,
my feeble fancy's listless flight
can never capture, I acknowledge,
the merest shadow of Thy light;
but hast Thou need of exaltation?
No mortal's pale imagination
could craft a song fit for Thine ears,
but must instead—to Thee aspiring,
Thy boundless variance admiring—
pour forth, before Thee, grateful tears.

Translated from the Russian by Alexander Levitsky

Ann Griffiths (1776–1805) was a Welsh Methodist hymn writer and poet. She was born into an Anglican family near the village of Llanfihangel-yng-Ngwynfa in northern Wales. Along with many others in her family, she later became a Methodist. She married a local farmer and died in childbirth at 29.

Expecting the Lord

Being myself so corrupted
With the forsaking life I lead,
To be on your holy mountain
Is high privilege indeed;
There the veils are rent, and coverings
Destroyed from that time forth,
And there is your excelling glory
On the transient things of earth.

O to keep at that high drinking
Where the streams of great salvation flow,
Till I'm utterly disthirsted
For the transient things below!
To live, and my Lord always expected!
To be, when he comes, up and awake!
Quick as a flash to open for him!
Enjoy him without stint or break!

Rose of Sharon

Look, between the myrtles standing
A true object of my thought—
Though I know only in part now
He surpasses the wordly sort,
    Yet, come morning,
I shall see him as he is.

His name is the Rose of Sharon;
He's white and ruddy, fair of worth;
He excels above ten thousand
Of the chief objects of earth;
    Friend to a sinner,
He's the pilot on the sea.

Why should I go any longer
To the poor idols at my feet?
None of their company, I swear it,
With my great Jesus can compete—
    Oh, if only
All my life stayed in his love!

Full of Wonder

Full of wonder, full of wonder for angels,
Faith can see great wonder in this—
Giver of being, abundant sustainer,
Governor of all that is,
In the manger a swaddled baby
Without a home to lay him in,
And still the bright hosts of glory
Are even now adoring him.

When Sinai's altogether smoking
And at its loudest the trumpet's cry,
Past the divide I can go feasting
In Christ the Word, and not die.
There in him dwells every fullness
To fill what man's perdition unmade;
He on the breach between the two parties
Offering himself, quittance paid.

He hung between thieves, who is Redemption,
Suffered death in anguish and loss;
Himself made strong the arms of hangmen
There to nail him on the cross;
Paying the debt of brands from the burning
He exalts justice (his father's law),
Forgives in terms of the free atonement
And justice, blazing, shines the more.

O my soul, look! Chief of kings, author
Of peace, he lay in that room,
The creation in him moving
And he a dead man in the tomb!
Song and life of the lost! Most wonder
Of all to angels and seraphim—
God in flesh, they see him and worship
Choirs of them shouting, "Be unto Him!"

Thanks, ten thousand times I thank him,
Thank him while I've breath and tongue,
For being what he is, to worship
And for ever be theme of song!
In this my nature he's been tempted
Like the least man that ever trod—
A small child, he was weak, was feeble,
Was infinite, true and living God.

To carry no more corruption's body,
Co-penetrate with the choirs above
Fiery into unending wonders
Of Calvary's redeeming love;
Live to behold him, the Invisible
Who died and now lives flesh and blood
In never-to-be-broken union
And co-union with my God.

I may exalt there the Name that Godhead
Put as atonement over the whole,
Nor shall veil or imagination
Block his true image from my soul.
In the fellowship of the mystery
Opened in the wound he bore,
To kiss the Son to everlasting
And turn my back on him no more!

Translated from the Welsh by Tony Conran

Translators

James Waddel Alexander (1804–1859) was an American Presbyterian minister and theologian.

Geoffrey Alan Argent is an independent scholar residing in Pennsylvania. He was the recipient of a 2011 American Book Award for *The Fratricides*, volume 1 of *The Complete Plays of Jean Racine* (Penn State, 2010).

William Baer is the author of twenty-eight books including *Luís de Camões: Selected Sonnets*; *Conversations with Derek Walcott*; and *Formal Salutations: New & Selected Poems*. A Guggenheim recipient, he has also received a Fulbright (Portugal) and an NEA Creative Writing Fellowship.

Sir Henry Williams Baker, 3rd Baronet (1821–1877) was an English Anglican clergyman and hymn writer.

Stanislaw Baranczak (1946–2014) was a poet, translator, and literary critic. He won the 2007 Nike Award and the 2009 Silesius Poetry Award. He was a professor of Polish language and literature at Harvard University.

Willis Barnstone, professor, poet, and scholar, is the author of over eighty volumes, including *The Restored New Testament*, *The Gnostic Bible*, *The Poems of Jesus Christ*, *The Poetics of Translation*, and *Mexico in My Heart: New and Selected Poems*. He lives in Oakland, California.

Sebastian P. Brock was, until his retirement in 2003, a reader in Syriac studies at the University of Oxford. He is the author of numerous books, including *The Bible in Syriac Tradition* and *An Outline of Syriac Literature*.

Poet, librettist, essayist, and translator, **Scott Cairns'** dozen books include *Slow Pilgrim: The Collected Poems* and *Anaphora*. A Guggenheim Fellow, he is the recipient of the Denise Levertov Award. He lives in Tacoma, Washington.

Bogdana Carpenter is professor emeritus of Slavic languages and literature and comparative literature at the University of Michigan. She is the author of *The Poetic Avant-Garde in Poland, 1918–1939* and *Monumenta Polonica: The First Four Centuries of Polish Poetry*, as well as other works.

JOHN CARPENTER is a poet and literary critic. He is the author of *Creating the World* and a study of the literature of the Second World War. Among the works the Carpenters have translated as a team are seven volumes of poetry and prose by Zbigniew Herbert.

EDWARD CASWALL (1814–1878) was an English Anglican clergyman and hymn writer who later converted to Roman Catholicism.

JONATHAN CHAVES is a scholar and translator of classical Chinese poetry. He has won the American Literary Translators Association award for best Asian translation, and been nominated for the National Book Award in the translation category.

CHRISTOPHER CHILDERS is a poet and translator living in Baltimore, MD. His *Penguin Book of Greek and Latin Lyric Verse* is forthcoming from Penguin Classics.

NOEL CLARK (1926–2004) was born in London and studied at Queen's College, Oxford. He worked for the BBC as a foreign correspondent and then as a freelance literary translator—mostly of classic plays in verse—from Polish, French, Dutch and German.

TONY CONRAN (1931–2013) was a leading Welsh poet, translator and critic. He taught for many years at Bangor University in northern Wales.

In addition to scholarly monographs and articles on Slavic subjects, HENRY R. COOPER, JR. has published numerous translations of Slovene, Croatian, and Serbian poetry and prose. He lives in Chicago.

WILLIAM JOHN COPELAND (1804–1885) was an English Anglican clergyman and scholar.

MARYANN CORBETT is an American poet, medievalist, and linguist. She is the author of five books of poetry and is a past winner of the Richard Wilbur Award and the Willis Barnstone Translation Prize. Her work appears in anthologies including Best American Poetry 2018. She lives in Saint Paul, Minnesota.

MARK DEGARMEAUX teaches at Bethany Lutheran College in Mankato, Minnesota. His translations include *Mother of the Reformation: The Amazing Life and Story of Katharine Luther*, four volumes of *U. V. Koren's Works*, and hundreds of Scandinavian hymns, mostly unpublished.

JOHN DENT-YOUNG is a freelance editor and translator who has also translated from Mandarin Chinese. He was a lecturer in English at the Chinese University of Hong Kong for nearly twenty years.

JOANNE EPP is the author of two poetry collections, *Eigenheim* (2015) and *Cattail Skyline* (2021). She lives in Winnipeg, where she serves as assistant organist at St. Margaret's Anglican Church.

ANTHONY M. ESOLEN is a professor of humanities and writer in residence, at Magdalen College of the Liberal Arts (Warner, NH). He has translated Lucretius, *On the Nature of Things*, and Tasso, *Jerusalem Delivered* (Johns Hopkins UP), Dante's *Divine Comedy* (Random House), and Riccardo Bacchelli, *The Gaze of Jesus* (Ignatius Press).

RHINA P. ESPAILLAT is an award-winning bilingual American poet. She was born in the Dominican Republic and came to New York City with her family due to the increasing brutality of the Trujillo regime. She taught for many years in the New York City Public School system and now lives in Newburyport, Massachusetts.

Acclaimed for her best-selling translations of Cervantes, Gabriel García Márquez, and Mario Vargas Llosa, **EDITH GROSSMAN** has received many awards including the PEN/Ralph Manheim Medal for Translation. She lives in New York City.

MARY T. HANSBURY (1942–2021) taught at La Salle University in Philadelphia and at Bethlehem University in Palestine. She received her Ph.D. from Temple University with additional work done in Jewish studies at Hebrew University and Syriac at Princeton University.

SEAMUS HEANEY (1939–2013) received the Nobel Prize in Literature in 1995. His poems, plays, translations, and essays include *Opened Ground*, *Electric Light*, *Beowulf*, *The Spirit Level*, *District and Circle*, and *Finders Keepers*.

FREDERIC HENRY HEDGE (1805–1890) was an American Unitarian minister and Transcendentalist.

GERARD MANLEY HOPKINS (1844–1889) was an English poet and Jesuit priest.

BURL HORNIACHEK is a Canadian poet and translator. He lives in Selkirk, Manitoba, with his wife and two children.

E.J. HUTCHINSON is Associate Professor of Classics at Hillsdale College, where he also directs the Collegiate Scholars Program.

SALLY ITO is a poet and translator living in Winnipeg. Her first book of translated poetry, with co-translator Michiko Tsuboi, was *Are You an Echo: The Lost Poetry of Misuzu Kaneko*, published in 2016 by Chin Music Press.

RENÉ B. JAVELLANA is Associate Professor of Fine Arts at the Ateneo de Manila University, Philippines. His research is on the historical sources of Philippine vernacular literature and the visual arts.

JOHN ALBERT JEFFREY (1855–1929) was an English hymn writer.

RICHARD JONES is the author of many books of poems, including the recent *Avalon* (Green Linden Press), *Paris* (Tebot Bach Books) and *Stranger on Earth* (Copper Canyon Press). He is the editor of *Poetry East* and curates its various anthologies, including *London*, *Cosmos*, and *Bliss*.

JOHN KELLY (1833–1890) was a British Presbyterian minister.

SARAH KLASSEN was born in Winnipeg and grew up in Manitoba's Interlake. An accomplished traveller, poet and fiction writer, her work has won numerous awards.

MISCHA KUDIAN (1918–1997) was a British writer, translator, painter and dentist who specialised in English renderings of Armenian literature, for which he set up the imprint Mashtots Press in the early 1970s.

CLIVE LAWRENCE was born in 1969 and graduated from Cambridge in 1990. He has worked in the legal profession since 1991. In 2011 he was joint winner of the John Dryden Prize, for his translations of Ronsard.

ALEXANDER LEVITSKY is a native of Prague. In 1964, he became a political refugee and eventually made his way to the U.S. He is Professor Emeritus of Slavic Studies at Brown University, where he taught for 40 years.

RALPH LEE has worked in Ethiopia for a total of 16 years teaching both chemical engineering and theology in Ethiopia. Since returning to the UK he has taught and supervised research at SOAS, Cambridge, and within the Cambridge Theological Federation.

TRANSLATORS

Henry Wadsworth Longfellow (1807–1882) was an American poet and university professor.

John A. McGuckin is the Nielsen Professor Emeritus of Early Church History at Union Theological Seminary, now serving in the Theology Faculty of Oxford University. He is an Archpriest of the Orthodox Church.

Adrian Mitchell (1932–2008) was an English playwright, poet and activist. He worked with the Royal Shakespeare Company, the National Theatre and the Unicorn Theatre, and his plays have been performed across the world.

Anthony Mortimer is emeritus professor of English Literature at the University of Fribourg, Switzerland. In addition to his academic work, he has published ten volumes of poetry translated from Italian, French and German.

Mark Musa (1934–2014) was Distinguished Professor of Italian at Indiana University. He is known for his translations of the Italian classics, including Dante, Petrarch, Boccaccio and Machiavelli.

John Mason Neale (1818–1866) was an English Anglican clergyman, scholar and hymnwriter. Among his most famous hymns is *Good King Wenceslas*.

John Frederick Nims (1913-1999) was the author of eight books of poetry, including *Knowledge of the Evening*, which was nominated for a National Book Award. He was editor of *Poetry* magazine from 1978 to 1984.

Frank O'Connor was born in Cork, Ireland, in 1903. Although best known as a short story writer, he also wrote novels, literary criticism, and translated many poems from the Irish. He died in Dublin in 1966.

Ewald Osers (1917–2011) was an internationally acclaimed literary translator from German, Czech and other Slavonic languages, including the poetry of Nobel Prize winner Jaroslav Seifert. Born in Czechoslovakia, he came to UK in 1938 and worked for the BBC, as well as writing his own poetry.

Besides her two-volume edition of Campanella's *Selected Philosophical Poems*, **Sherry Roush** has translated works by Nicolò Franco, Piovano Arlotto, and Girolamo Benivieni among others; her current project — Jacopo

Caviceo's *Peregrino* (1508) — received NEA and NEH grants. She is a Professor of Italian at Penn State University.

JOSEPH S. SALEMI teaches in the Department of Classical Languages at Hunter College in New York City. He is a widely published scholar, essayist, and translator, and he edits the poetry magazine *TRINACRIA*.

THOMAS J. SAMUELIAN is an American-Armenian linguist and author of a number of books and articles in the field of Armenian language, literature, and history. He is currently Dean of the College of Humanities & Social Sciences, American University of Armenia.

R. J. SCHORK is Professor Emeritus of Classics at the University of Massachusetts, Boston, and the author of more than 60 articles on ancient and modern literature, as well as books on the influence of Greek and Latin culture on James Joyce.

MICHAEL SMITH was born in Dublin in 1942. He was well-known for his poetry, his editorial work, his translations of Spanish poetry (many with Luis Ingelmo), and his polemical support for the lost generation of Irish modernist poets. He died in 2014.

A.E. STALLINGS is a US-born poet living in Greece. Her most recent poetry collection, *Like* (FSG), was a finalist for the Pulitzer Prize. Her most recent verse translation is the (illustrated) pseudo-Homeric *Battle Between the Frogs and Mice* with Paul Dry Books. A selected poems, *This Afterlife*, is now out with FSG (US) and Carcanet (UK).

JOSUAH SYLVESTER (1563–1618) was an English poet and translator.

GEORGE SZIRTES is a poet and translator. He was born in Budapest in 1948, and came to England after the 1956 Hungarian uprising. His collection *Reel* won the TS Eliot prize in 2004; his latest book is *Fresh Out of the Sky* (2022).

HENRY VAUGHAN (1621–1695) was a Welsh poet, prose writer, translator and physician.

RICHARD WILBUR (1921-2017) served as poet laureate of the United States. He received the National Book Award, two Pulitzer Prizes, the National Arts Club medal of honor for literature, and a number of translation prizes, including two Bollingen Prizes and two awards from PEN.

Rowan Williams was Archbishop of Canterbury from 2002 to 2012 and Master of Magdalene College, Cambridge, from 2013 to 2020. He is well-known as a theologian, and has also published several collections of poetry. He collaborated with Gwyneth Lewis in translating the *Book of Taliesin* for Penguin Classics in 2018.

Catherine Winkworth (1827–1878) was an English Unitarian hymn-writer and advocate for women's education.

Jan Zwicky's most recent book is *The Experience of Meaning*. She lives on the west coast of Canada.

Acknowledgments

"Hymn XII" from *Hymns of Paradise* by St. Ephrem the Syrian, translated by Sebastian Brock, translation copyright © 1997 by St. Vladimir's Seminary Press. Reprinted by permission of St. Vladimir's Seminary Press.

Excerpts from *On the Mother of God* by Jacob of Serug, translated by Mary Hansbury, translation copyright © 1998 by St. Vladimir's Seminary Press. Reprinted by permission of St. Vladimir's Seminary Press.

"A Solis Ortus Cardine" by Sedulius, translated by E.J. Hutchinson, first appeared in Ad Fontes Journal. Reprinted by permission of the translator.

Romanos the Melodist, Sacred Song from the Byzantine Pulpit, by R. J. Schork. Gainesville: University Press of Florida, 1995, pp. 162-175, 209-219. Reprinted by permission of the University Press of Florida.

"Concerning a Nightingale" by Alcuin, translated by Maryann Corbett, is reprinted by permission of the translator.

"A Prayer for Recollection" and "A Priest Rediscovers His Psalm-Book," translated by Frank O'Connor, are reprinted by permission of the translator's estate.

"Prayer 12" and "Prayer 46" from *The Book of Lamentations* by Gregory of Narek, translated by Thomas J. Samuelian, are reprinted by permission of the translator.

Excerpt from *Jesus the Son* by St. Nerses IV the Gracious, translated by Mischa Kudian, translation copyright © 1970 by Mashtots Press. Reprinted by permission of the Armenian Institute.

Saint Francis of Assisi: "His Blessings and His Praise" from *Endless Life: Poems of the Mystics* by Scott Cairns © 2007 by Scott Cairns. Reprinted by permission of Paraclete Press.

Excerpt from *Purgatory* by Dante Alighieri, translated by Anthony Esolen, translation copyright © 2003 by Penguin Random House LLC. Used by permission of Modern Library, an imprint of Random House, a division of Penguin Random House LLC. All rights reserved.

The Poiema Poetry Series

COLLECTIONS IN THIS SERIES INCLUDE:

Six Sundays Toward a Seventh by Sydney Lea

Epitaphs for the Journey by Paul Mariani

Within This Tree of Bones by Robert Siegel

Particular Scandals by Julie L. Moore

Gold by Barbara Crooker

A Word In My Mouth by Robert Cording

Say This Prayer into the Past by Paul Willis

Scape by Luci Shaw

Conspiracy of Light by D.S. Martin

Second Sky by Tania Runyan

Remembering Jesus by John Leax

What Cannot Be Fixed by Jill Pelaez Baumgaertner

Still Working It Out by Brad Davis

The Hatching of the Heart by Margo Swiss

Collage of Seoul by Jae Newman

Twisted Shapes of Light by William Jolliff

These Intricacies by David Harrity

Where the Sky Opens by Laurie Klein

True, False, None of the Above by Marjorie Maddox

The Turning Aside anthology edited by D.S. Martin

Falter by Marjorie Stelmach

Phases by Mischa Willett

Second Bloom by Anya Krugovoy Silver

Adam, Eve, & the Riders of the Apocalypse anthology edited by D.S. Martin

Your Twenty-First Century Prayer Life by Nathaniel Lee Hansen

Habitation of Wonder by Abigail Carroll

Ampersand by D.S. Martin

Full Worm Moon by Julie L. Moore

Ash & Embers by James A. Zoller

The Book of Kells by Barbara Crooker

Reaching Forever by Philip C. Kolin

The Book of Bearings by Diane Glancy

In a Strange Land anthology edited by D.S. Martin

What I Have I Offer With Two Hands by Jacob Stratman

Slender Warble by Susan Cowger

Madonna, Complex by Jen Stewart Fueston

No Reason by Jack Stewart

Abundance by Andrew Lansdown

Angelicus by D.S. Martin

Trespassing on the Mount of Olives by Brad Davis

The Angel of Absolute Zero by Marjorie Stelmach

Duress by Karen An-hwei Lee

Wolf Intervals by Graham Hillard